Praise for *Finding Yourself in the Kitchen*:

"A quietly brilliant ode to the myriad pleasures—both mundane and sublime—to be discovered in the daily ritual of cooking. Dana Velden's words read like a deliciously warm hug to cooks of all ilks; her charming stories, appealing recipes, meditative reflections, and honest encouragement will lure hesitant newbies to the stove and remind seasoned cooks why they fell in love with the kitchen in the first place."

—*Erin Scott, author of* Yummy Supper

"*Finding Yourself in the Kitchen* is a glorious meditation on the quiet magnificence of the mundane, and how kitchen tasks—everything from cooking to cleaning to placing a simple bowl of lemons on your kitchen table—can root and ground us in a noisy world that is distracting and nebulous. This is an instant classic, and a must-have addition to my kitchen bookshelf where I predict it will remain forever, dog-eared, stained, falling apart, and deeply loved."

—*Elissa Altman, author of* Poor Man's Feast: A Love Story of Comfort, Desire, and the Art of Simple Cooking

"The way Dana articulates what happens in the kitchen has helped me form my own deep-rooted philosophies about the cooking life. I turn to her when I cannot find the words to express how utterly healing and ultimately metaphorical it is to pick up a knife or stir a pot of soup. I am so grateful that she finally put what I am sure is just a fraction of her rich experience into a collection of chapters for us all to experience."

—*Sara Kate Gillingham, James Beard Award-winning cookbook author and cofounder of TheKitchn.com*

"Every great cook I've known has one thing in common: She is a master observer. *Finding Yourself in the Kitchen* is a beautiful paean to paying attention in the kitchen, which is as essential to good cooking as olive oil and salt. With grace and sensitivity, it will inspire you to find new joy and meaning in cooking by simply being present."

—*Samin Nosrat, writer and chef*

Finding Yourself in the Kitchen

Finding Yourself in the Kitchen

Kitchen Meditations *and* Inspired Recipes from a Mindful Cook

DANA VELDEN

contributor to *The Kitchn*

RODALE.

We inspire and enable people to improve their lives and the world around them.
rodalebooks.com

This book is dedicated to the readers of my
Weekend Meditation *posts on* The Kitchn.
*Without your cajoling and encouragement, I would
not have had the confidence and courage to create
a book. You believed, and so then I believed,
and that's how this came to be.*

CONTENTS

INTIMACY, PART 1: THE TANGIBLE WORLD

INTIMACY, PART 2: A STATE OF MIND

You Reading This, Be Ready

WILLIAM STAFFORD

Starting here, what do you want to remember?
How sunlight creeps along a shining floor?
What scent of old wood hovers, what softened
sound from outside fills the air?

Will you ever bring a better gift for the world
than the breathing respect that you carry
wherever you go right now? Are you waiting
for time to show you some better thoughts?

When you turn around, starting here, lift this
new glimpse that you found; carry into evening
all that you want from this day. This interval you spent
reading or hearing this, keep it for life—

What can anyone give you greater than now,
starting here, right in this room, when you turn around?

INTRODUCTION

SEVERAL years ago, when I was in my midthirties, my life fell apart and I went to live in a Zen Buddhist monastery deep in the wild mountains of northern California. In the mornings and evenings, I would sit for hours in meditation with my fellow monks and in the afternoons, we would work. I often ended up in the kitchen, which suited me just fine, although sometimes I cleaned the bathhouse or dug ditches or picked flowers for the altars.

Divorce, the death of my father, and a difficult surgery had left me torn apart and shaken. Little by little, by giving myself over to meditation and the monastery work, and especially my time in the kitchen, I began to knit myself together and grow back—not perfect and new, but stronger and somehow more myself.

Zen kitchens are often strict, silent places. There's a top-down hierarchy, and the request is to just do the task that you are given with no preferences. Of course, I had many, many preferences and opinions. I preferred chopping carrots to washing kale and tearing lettuce, and I especially loved it when it was my turn to make the soup for lunch. But even if I was given the soup, the culture of that kitchen dictated that it wasn't about my ideas of what the soup should be. I couldn't add caraway to the carrot soup, for instance, without consulting the head cook, and usually the head cook would raise her eyebrow slightly and gently say: "Please, just follow the recipe." Still, the act of cooking, even if it was simply following the recipe, had enough decision-making activity to feel creative and even a little exciting.

But eventually, I found that while the soup-making task had its (somewhat-limited) creative expression, the chopping and tearing and washing chores were also expressive and there was enjoyment in these simple, repetitive tasks. There was freedom, too, in the realization that always getting what I thought I wanted or what I believed I liked wasn't going to bring me lasting pleasure. So I learned to stop chasing my desires and to settle more deeply into myself and the rhythms of monastic life. Soon I discovered that the greatest joy ultimately came not from getting my preferences met but in responding to whatever request was in front of me. If carrot coins were needed, then I filled the 2-gallon pail next to me with bright orange rounds, each whole carrot different and requiring my attention to produce the ½-inch size requested by the head cook. Is it time for dishes? Then okay, we'll do the dishes or sweep the floor or sauté the onions in oil until soft.

Zen kitchens are also highly structured and exacting places. On the wall above the lettuce-washing sink in that mountain temple kitchen, there was a small framed and slightly waterlogged pen-and-ink drawing of a fish and the handwritten words "Like a fish in a puddle, what pleasure is there here?" What pleasure indeed? While at times enormously challenging, the kitchen was also a tight container, which had its comforts and in a very odd way, its freedoms. It was exactly what I needed to hold me together, to help me to mend and grow whole again. Was it always pleasurable? Of course not. But my time there had moments of exquisite joy, and it certainly presented me with opportunities to grow and develop strength and endurance.

There was beauty to be found, too, in the most basic of things, if only I would remember to open my eyes and look: A bucketful of compost scraps, the bright explosion of red radishes and orange slices tossed together to garnish a salad, the way the sunlight came in and lit up the pile of dishes drying by the window. As my time in the monastery lengthened, a deep quiet settled inside me, and I began to experience my life from a place of stillness. This experience wasn't necessarily soft and gentle. It had a rugged quality to it that felt up to the demands of a human life. And the pain place, while it never left completely (it never does), took a step back and stopped calling all the shots.

Zen kitchens have taught me so much: how a deep contentment is cultivated when I focus my attention on the task at hand; how to care about something without grasping at it; how to allow the bright world to come forth and show me what was needed; and how responding to that need was a great and powerful form of love. They taught me about the practicalities of cleaning up my messes, how to hold a knife so that I could chop onions for an hour straight, and the best way to dress a salad. I learned how to work elbow-to-elbow with someone who gave me difficulty and how to engage with that difficulty in a way that took care of the problem, and the both of us, and the people around us.

———•—•—•———

At this point you may be wondering what kind of book is this? Is it a cookbook? In some ways it is and in some ways it isn't. If a cookbook is a technical manual for conveying a formula (recipes), then the answer is no, this is not just a cookbook. There are a few recipes here and there, sure, because the form and structure of recipes are helpful, just like a stop sign on a busy corner is helpful. Recipes are essential for most beginning cooks and are terrific starting places for more experienced ones. Besides, recipes are fun! But more than recipes, or perhaps beyond the recipes, this book is an encouragement to allow yourself the opportunity to be curious and engaged with the food you prepare and eat, and with the place—the kitchen—where it all happens.

For more than 6 years now, I have written the Sunday post on a food blog called *The Kitchn*. When I started, the editors gave it the title *Weekend Meditation* and brief instructions to write about the more thoughtful aspects of food, cooking, and life in the kitchen. My first post was about washing dishes: how to bring attention to this everyday chore and the possibility of enjoyment to be found there. Now, more than 300 *Weekend Meditations* later, I continue to be surprised to find that this subject, this idea that the whole of our lives can be expressed in what we do, is inexhaustible. Each week I think, "How can there be anything more to say?" And each week, there is always something. From that exploration this book grew and took on its own related but independent mission: to encourage you to find out what happens when you open your eyes and engage with whatever is in front of you, right here, right now.

There is perhaps nothing more mundane than the two or three meals a day an average kitchen produces. This is important. We can get swept away by the drama of the "inspired kitchen," but equally important is the bare, bold fact that much of life is routine, plain, and uneventful. We make the same toast for breakfast or always have vegetarian food on Mondays. We endlessly chop onions and peel potatoes and wipe down that same counter over and over again. It's not easy to stay engaged when a task is repetitive, when it's not exciting or sexy. So, ultimately, more than anything, what I think we need is encouragement. We need to be encouraged and supported to step into the kitchen as a place of discovery, a place to uncover and loosen the knots that keep us too safe and distant and somehow not fully in our lives.

Inspiration is also important. And by inspiration I mean that energized feeling you get that causes you to put down whatever you're doing and get into the kitchen. It could be to tackle something new or a remake of your tried-and-true. You could resolve to finally get over your lifelong fear of yeast baking or reconnect with your grandmother over her plum torte recipe. Whatever it is, there is a woken-up quality to it that feels both connected and vital. This vitality is the nourishment we take in to remain curious and on our toes, deeply and happily involved in the process of being alive. To do this, we must be agile. We must engage the world with clear eyes and our simple, bare presence. Presence, more than any knife skill or recipe collection, is the most important thing in the kitchen and indeed in a human life. It's an essential part of the mixture (breath, food, purpose, love, and belonging) that keeps us alive.

———————

I no longer live at the San Francisco Zen Center or work in those Zen kitchens, but I've settled nearby and still maintain close, important relationships with the people I know there and the meditation practice we share. When I started writing this book, I was surprised and delighted to discover that while I may have left the Zen kitchen, the Zen kitchen apparently has never left me. The lessons of focus, attention, appreciation, and intimacy are still with me, almost as if they are marbled throughout my being and have spilled out across these pages.

So this book, while not strictly or overtly a Zen book, is deeply anchored in those years spent in Zen kitchens. Maybe it will inspire you to spend some time of your own in a Zen kitchen; but even more, I hope that you can find its teachings in the very kitchen you have right now. You really don't have to lose everything and travel to a remote valley to discover that the world is always rushing forward to teach us, and that the greatest thing we can do is to stand there, open and available, and be taught by it. There is no limit to what this cracked and broken and achingly beautiful world can offer, and there is equally no limit to our ability to meet it.

Each day, the sun rises and we get out of bed. Another day has begun and bravely, almost recklessly, we stagger into it not knowing what it will bring to us. How will we meet this unpredictable, untamable human life? How will we answer its many questions and challenges and delights? What will we do when we find ourselves, stumble over ourselves, encounter ourselves, once again, in the kitchen?

On Why I Wrote This Book

IT'S early on a cold and foggy October morning in Oakland, California. I'm sitting at my kitchen table, a cup of hot tea clutched in both hands, pondering the last of the garden tomatoes that are rolling around on a platter in front of me. Summer is pretty much over, so they're smaller and maybe a little tougher in skin but still sweet and worthy of one final raw tomato salad. Later in October, autumn will have completely taken hold with its rough and tumble of squash and knobby quince and fat, oval persimmons. But today, it's the last of the tomatoes, and I have to admit that I'm a little sad about saying goodbye.

Early October is often a tender, vulnerable time for me when I feel the weight of my life more keenly, and all my joys and sorrows and challenges and pleasures seem to register in a deeper place. It's a time of transition, both exciting and unsettling, and I find even more than ever that the kitchen is a place for refuge. I want to linger here, as I am this morning, and consider the tomatoes. I want to narrow my focus, quiet my mind, and concern myself with the immediacy and intimacy of the simplest, most basic thing we do: feeding ourselves, feeding others.

Cooking is a grounding activity for me. It consists mostly of everyday, mundane things like chopping and peeling and washing up. And dinner is often simply just dinner, a meal I will have nearly every day for the rest of my life. Thousands and thousands of dinners behind me and thousands and thousands of dinners ahead (maybe . . . hopefully!). If I want to serve and eat fresh, healthy food, then I have to make peace with the mundane, even monotonous work of the kitchen. This isn't as hard as it sounds. It actually can be quite pleasant if I can give over to the task at hand and stop fighting with it. Just work with one potato, one onion, one dirty dish at a time.

So yes, there are chores when we cook but, at the same time, cooking also allows for creativity and curiosity because every day there's something new to explore. Modern folk tend to forget this, but our ingredients are for the most part from the natural world and therefore they are never the same one day to the next, one shopping trip to the next. How to cook this potato, this particular variety, this particular size, on this particular day? Has it been in storage or dug fresh from the ground? Am I hungry for something warm and fluffy (mashed) or creamy and golden (gratin)? Will this be the focus of my meal or a supporting side? Do I have garlic in the house? Is there room in the oven? How much time do I have?

———·—·—·——

When we cook, we are expressing ourselves completely, for we always cook within the context of our lives. If we're stretched for cash this week, if we're feeling lonely, stressed, generous, too busy, happy—whatever is happening in that moment—when we step up to the stove, we cook with these circumstances as much as any ingredient or recipe. This kind of attention to the particulars of the moment won't be found in the recipe we are using, yet it will have an enormous influence on the final product and how much enjoyment we will receive from both the doing and the consuming of it.

I want to encourage and support us to look more deeply, and experience more deeply, our everyday lives. I feel . . . no actually, I know . . . there is a hunger today for a more considered life, one where our everyday circumstances are not a series of inconveniences to get through (or around) as quickly as possible but rather a source of our awakening and pleasure. We don't have to go looking for it, we don't have to purchase it, because it's right here: in the way a cup of tea warms our hands, in the contemplation of the last of summer tomato, in the rough skin of a storage potato, the scent of garlic softening in oil.

I believe that we have plenty of cookbooks and websites and classes and streaming videos to show us the mechanics of cooking. What we have very little of is instruction on how to discover and work with the more internal aspects of being in the kitchen: how to awaken curiosity, how to work with boredom, what cooking can teach us about mistakes, failure, beauty, and intimacy. I wrote this book to take up this less examined side of cooking, to encourage and inspire a more deeply experienced life, and to help us discover that no matter what the circumstances, we all have the capacity to deeply nourish ourselves and those around us.

———·———·———·———

The last summer tomatoes ended up in an epic BLT lunch. Nothing fancy. But the whole process, from the moment they were handed to me from a green-thumbed friend, to their appearance on my kitchen table, to my morning contemplation, and finally to their starring role in my lunch, was immensely satisfying. The particular kind of satisfaction that comes when we pause, take stock, and discover that, often, everything we need is right at hand.

The First Thing: Mornings, Tea, and Meditation

Leave your front door and your back door open. Allow your thoughts to come and go. Just don't serve them tea.

—Suzuki Roshi, Zen monk and teacher, on how to meditate

THIS morning, like every morning, I got up and went into my kitchen to make a cup of tea. While the water was heating, I quietly put away the dishes left over from last night's washing up and brushed a few stray crumbs off of the counter and into the dustbin. Soon the tea was ready: a good strong, hot cup of breakfast blend barely tamed with a splash of milk. Moving onto a chair in my living room, I spent the next 10 minutes or so just sitting quietly, taking small quick sips of the hot tea, and watching whatever happened to wander into my mind.

This is my morning ritual, a kind of teacup meditation. The rules are simple: It's okay to think but not to plan or leap ahead into the day. No strategizing, no ruminating on past hurts, no bright and jangly thoughts. Just a cup of tea and the simple act of noticing whatever appears.

Of course, planning and ruminating and strategizing thoughts can be a part of what appears, sometimes quite powerfully. And other times, even though it's early morning and the day hasn't formed yet, I'm already at sixes and sevens and restless as a baby Chihuahua. My effort, if there is any, is to not engage with these thoughts and energies. I'll have plenty of time later to consider the state of my bank account balance or how long it's been since my last dental cleaning or whether there will be rutabagas at the market for tonight's dinner.

Most mornings, my thinking is soft and based on immediate observations. I may notice the sunlight is arriving earlier and that it has shifted so it streams in directly through the window, or that the birdsong has slowed and mellowed now that the early days of spring are almost over. Some mornings, I might hear the clang and clamor of the garbage collection or the urgent but inconsequential chattering of an early dog walker on his cell phone. I might notice a whiff of lingering garlic and pimentón from last night's chorizo or how the dust has continued to accumulate on the baseboards.

Whatever it is, I try for a state of observation, not opinion. I try to engage in the present and not the past or future. I try to just notice and appreciate whatever this particular morning is bringing forward. I have the entire remaining day to form opinions and take action. There are more than enough hours in my life devoted to doing. These early moments are for the rare and precious state of just being.

Ten or so minutes later, my tea is gone and I'm a little more awake, a little more in my skin, and a little more ready to step out into the impossible task, the enormous privilege, of living a human life.

This is a practice that I do every day. I highly recommend it.

Eight Simple Things to Do to Be Happy in Your Kitchen

SEVERAL years ago I wrote a post for *The Kitchn* called "Ten Simple Things to Make You Happier in Your Kitchen." It was a popular post, with many people chiming in via the comments section to add their own take on kitchen happiness. In reading it over recently, I realized that much of what I wrote then still applies for me today.

Here's a slightly revised version of that list. I hope it inspires you to consider what makes you happy in your kitchen. If you don't know or have never considered this question, take a moment to find out. Pay attention to when you're happiest in your kitchen. Take note of the causes and conditions that help to create this feeling and be sure to practice and celebrate them as often as possible.

1. Keep a well-stocked pantry. A well-stocked pantry is fundamental in any kitchen, no matter what our aspirations are for happiness. So it's important to give our pantries enough attention and consideration. When it comes to nonperishables, there's no reason not to keep the cupboard shelves as overflowing as space and budget will allow so that at any given time, we can walk into the kitchen and create a decent meal for ourselves or an unexpected guest.

What we keep in our pantries (and refrigerators, for that matter) is a very personal reflection of who we are as cooks. The items reflect our interests and abilities, our income, food culture, space limitations, and time constraints. These are the things we reach for without thinking too much and have no problem remembering to restock when needed. The basics.

It's also important to stock things for a favorite dish or a particular category of food or cuisine. These items are very specific: a certain kind of fish sauce, for example. Or a selection of different kinds of flours for bread-baking. We may not use these items every day but having them on hand means we're more apt to break free of our routine and have some fun every now and then.

I also like to think of cooking time and convenience when I'm stocking my pantry so that there are a variety of things available that can be cooked up quickly as well as things that work for longer, slower projects. So for example, my legume area has canned beans (short cooking time), lentils (medium cooking time), and dried beans (long cooking time.)

It is also important to have a few unknowns in your pantry, a wildcard item or two that inspires you to cook outside your usual habits. I try to pick up one small but new-to-me ingredient every now and then. This could be as simple as an unusual variety of dried bean or as exotic as a jar of dried Iranian limes.

2. Grow fresh herbs in pots. I don't think I've ever met a devoted cook who doesn't believe in having fresh herbs on hand. As a black-thumbed gardener, this is a challenge for me as I have a hard time keeping plants alive. But I persist because I am quite convinced of the benefit of fresh herbs. They add a freshness and flavor that is impossible to duplicate (dried herbs and fresh herbs are not always interchangeable). So if at all possible, try growing some herbs in pots, either in a sunny kitchen window or very near to your kitchen door outside. You will be amazed by how much they will inspire you: A snip here and there, and suddenly you're off in a whole new direction!

If it is impossible to grow herbs in your home, purchase them from the farmers' market or grocery store and keep them in water on your counter. Treat them much like fresh flowers by trimming their stems and changing the water frequently. If your kitchen is warm, they may do better in the refrigerator, still in water and their leafy tops loosely draped in a plastic bag.

3. (Sort of) embrace the clutter. While we can admire the sleek, streamlined, nearly empty kitchens we see in blogs and magazines, the truth is that most home kitchens have a lot more going on in them if they are truly being used. Between those half-empty packets of pasta and eight kinds of vinegar, not to mention the myriad utensils needed to whisk, flip, beat, strain, measure, cut, grate, squeeze, shred, and stir our meals, we tend to accumulate a lot of stuff. And since a lot of stuff can quickly pile up, to a certain extent we need to embrace and work with clutter in our kitchens.

However you manage this and what it looks like is completely up to you. Maybe you have the space to stash it all away behind closed doors or maybe you're more of an out-of-sight, out-of-mind kind of cook and need to keep things visible. Whatever your style is, it's always more pleasant to cook in a clean kitchen with lots of available counter space with equipment and utensils in their proper place. So if you find that you just can't avoid the clutter, keep it as organized as possible and don't be afraid to purge every now and then.

4. Love your stuff. I will go into this more extensively later in the book but it bears repeating: It's important that you enjoy using the tools of your kitchen. If you sigh with displeasure every time you reach for that wobbly, dented frying pan, then your cooking experience with it is always going to be lacking. Invest in a few good pieces of kitchen equipment and plan on maintaining them for the rest of your life. (Better yet, keep a lookout at your local thrift store and yard sales. It's astonishing what people get rid of.) But no matter how or where you get it, or even its quality for that matter, if you really like a particular piece of kitchen equipment, you will use it often and you will use it with pleasure.

5. Try Deborah Madison's pan of warm, sudsy water. In an interview, the brilliant cook and cookbook author Deborah Madison once recommended filling the kitchen sink full of warm, soapy water before starting on a recipe. This is one of my favorite pieces of kitchen advice for it is practical and sensual and calming all at the same time. Washing my utensils as I use them is a pragmatic thing to do, but it also feels really wonderful to plunge my hands into warm, soapy water and clean off any stickiness or mess. And knowing that the tablespoon I just used and quickly cleaned will be ready for the next thing relieves some of the stress and confusion that can come with cooking, too. Extra points for using a pleasant-smelling dish soap!

6. Keep sharp knives. Having sharp knives in your kitchen will make a world of difference in your cooking. Contrary to what cookware stores tell you, you don't need a lot of them, so spend your money on quality over quantity. A simple chef's knife and a paring knife or two are a good place to start. If possible, hold the knife first before you purchase it to be sure it fits your hand and isn't too heavy for your wrist.

If you've been living with dull knives, gather them up and get them professionally sharpened—you will be amazed at how much more pleasant it is to chop and prep. And it's not that hard to keep them that way, so no excuses! Start with a professional sharpening, if needed, and maintain them by using a honing tool each time you pick up a knife. The honing tool won't sharpen a dull blade but it will help keep a sharpened blade sharp.

Equally important are cutting surfaces. Wood boards are best and most popular; plastic will also work, although plastic is not as sanitary as wood. The most important thing is to keep your boards very clean and toss out any that are severely scuffed up as they will tend to harbor bacteria. It also helps to have a few sizes available to match the task at hand.

7. Learn techniques, not recipes. I have nothing against recipes, but when it comes to being able to play in the kitchen—to experience the freedom to improvise and turn on a dime, if needed, then having an understanding of basic cooking techniques is far more important. These techniques can be as simple as knife skills and as complicated as understanding sauces and emulsions, but they are essential if you want to go beyond following a recipe.

Understanding fundamental techniques will free you up to experiment and allow you to feed a group of people a delicious meal with nothing more than a sack of potatoes and a few pantry items. It's not that hard to get started, especially with the Internet as a source for videos. Even better, take a class or ask a friend to show you the ropes. In the kitchen, as well as in life, never assume you're finished with learning. Always be teachable.

8. Pause and breathe. If you're in the kitchen and you're wired and stressed, pause and take a few breaths to see if you can't find a little calm in the middle of the chaos. If you're in the kitchen and you're happy as a lark, then pause and take a few breaths to let it all in, to really steep yourself in your enjoyment. If you're in the kitchen and you're bored, pause and take a breath, noticing what might be a little different about today's task at hand. No matter what your circumstances, pause and breathe. Look for where the sunlight is coming in, or notice the particular texture or color of the ingredient you are working with. Sniff the air. Every moment is endlessly fascinating and equally as fleeting. Don't let it slip away.

Be as seasonal as possible. This is my bonus recommendation. To the extent that you can, try to eat seasonally. As a wealthy nation, Americans have a belief that happiness means that we get what we want, whenever we want it. But I have found the opposite is true. When I have to wait for asparagus season to arrive, my delight is made so much sweeter by my anticipation and, of course, the asparagus itself is sweeter when it's in season and fresh from the ground. I find that when I'm living within the rhythms of the seasons, I have less anxiety, and I can clearly see where and how I am sustained. This connection, this acknowledgment—that even though I am living in a crowded urban area, I am still closely bound to the earth—is a never-ending source of comfort and joy.

The Three Intimacies

THE kitchen, perhaps more than any other room in our home, offers us many opportunities to discover intimacy. First, we experience intimacy with the tangible world through working with our bodies, our ingredients, and the physical space of our kitchen. Second, we explore intimacy as a state of mind and discover the degree to which we allow, or don't allow, the world and all its pleasures and pains to come in. And finally, there is the intimacy that we experience with others when we feed and nourish our friends and family and maybe even the occasional stranger.

This intimacy in all of its manifestations is serious business, for to be intimate is to allow something (or everything!) to make contact with us, to touch and therefore change us, often in ways we cannot predict or understand or control. Of course, we need to have some protections, for to run out into the world with no filter, with no shield against harm or difficulty, is a form of madness. But our protections can also be habitual and occasionally even neurotic. They may have been helpful at one point in our lives but maybe not so much in our current circumstances. Often, we've integrated that protective shield so well, so thoroughly, that we cannot undo it even when it's okay, even when it's perhaps better for us not to be so defended.

What brings us the most pleasure are the things that allow or encourage us to drop our protectiveness so that we can fully experience the moment, with no holding back. This is true whether our experience is moving or magnificent or quite ordinary. Sex is an obvious example, but so is listening to a favorite piece of music or completely losing ourselves to the task of making a soup. What makes these experiences so powerful is that we've let down our defenses and allowed the bare truth of the moment to come forward and touch us. We've allowed intimacy.

Sometimes, it's not even the content of the activity but simply the opportunity to drop our protectiveness, of being available to something outside of ourselves, that's the most compelling. The music is just the encouragement to lay down our defenses for a moment. The soup-making is so full of color and delicious smells and satisfying that we forget to be in our heads and instead slip into the hum of just being present, of trusting that the moment we are in will provide us with everything we need.

This is why I've structured this book by the three forms of intimacy: with the tangible world, as a state of mind, and with others. The world can be a scary and sometimes very dangerous place, but it is possible, and actually even necessary, for us to find refuge. To do this, we need to cultivate situations in our lives where we can discover and strengthen a sense of what is trustworthy: to trust our lives, to trust ourselves, and to trust what is coming forth and meet it without hesitation.

After the chrysanthemums,
Besides the daikon
There is nothing

BASHŌ

The Tangible World

SPENDING as much time as we do in the virtual world these days, it is possible that the beautiful, ordinary miracle of the physical world can become lost to us. Occasionally, we manage to lift up our heads, blinking and adjusting our sight to a point farther away than the screen, and it's like we've just woken up. It takes a moment or two to remember where we are and that we have a body, and that it is moving through space and time. The virtual world is alluring and it has its place and promise, but the actual world, the physical world, is still our most fundamental, necessary abode.

Because of this, one of the more modern reasons we cook is for the physicality of it, for the opportunity to turn toward and inhabit our bodies in this very real and basic way. After being in our heads all day, sitting around and thinking and typing on keyboards, we eventually grow restless and depleted. We feel unsatisfied and achy in our bones. What a joy it is, then, to turn away from our devices and go into the kitchen to rustle up some soup from a few onions and last night's chicken carcass. At last, something tangible, something practical, something that satisfies both the body and the spirit.

Cooking is compelling in part because of this physicality. It requires a kind of engagement that is both grounding and practical. Reading and discussing and analyzing a cake recipe will not make the cake. It simply must be done with our bodies, with actual ingredients and implements. We have no choice in this, really, so why not use the practical imperative to cook as a chance to deepen our engagement with our bodies and the world around us? Why not use our time in the kitchen like a counterweight against the ever-present distractions of our thinking and scheming and screen-gazing so that we can be pulled, almost without our knowing, into a more balanced way of being.

Of course, we can cook in a distracted manner, with our heads somewhere else and our bodies on autopilot. But cooking will quickly teach us that we need to be fully present and aware. There's a built-in, heightened sense of alertness when we cook, for the kitchen is fraught with the potential for failure and full of dangerous, sharp, hot, and heavy situations. One second of inattention and we've lost our way in a recipe (shit, did I already add the baking powder?) or missed the part about resting the dough overnight when making bread meant for tonight's dinner. If we want to be good cooks, successful cooks, then we have to pay attention. We have to be fully engaged and in the present moment or dinner won't make it to the table, or it won't be very delicious, or worse.

The Present Moment

People often talk about being in the present moment, sometimes throwing the phrase around as if it were a simple, basic task that anyone can do if they just try hard enough. As if somehow capturing each moment as it whizzes past is possible or even a desirable thing for a human being to do. But anyone who has tried to "be in the present moment" knows that the present moment is an elusive thing. Is it this moment or (a second later) is it this one? Wait, no, it's this one! Or maybe we determinedly vow to be in the present and then suddenly we pop out of a distracted reverie having completely missed the past 10 minutes.

One helpful way to look at it is that the present moment is less a thing that we apprehend and more a state of being that we can sink into. We find this not by trying to grab ahold of it, for that's like trying to hold on to a piece of water by plunging your hands into a moving stream. It is not something that can be done through will or determination. It's more about filling the mind with the act of noticing what is happening right here in front of you, right now. It's about cultivating the capacity for bare attention by stilling our active, thinking mind and allowing the present moment to arrive. It's about receptivity.

This isn't something that will come to us naturally or immediately for we are very accustomed to our distracted, daydreamy minds. (Or to our problem-solving, multitasking, just-one-step-in-front-of-disaster minds.) We are very good at thinking about what needs to happen in the future or getting caught up in what has happened in the past, so to do something different takes practice. Classic forms of meditation help to facilitate this by having us sit still and gaze at the wall or the ground in front of us, with the idea that it will minimize the amount of input and help us to settle down and focus. Which it does, often very well. But it also can provide us with a very large, very blank screen in which we can see, for better or worse, the relentlessness and veracity of our thoughts and inner workings. This can be far from settling, as I discussed previously in the morning tea meditation on page 28.

It's also true that unless we've managed to find ourselves in a monastery, it's doubtful that we will have the chance to sit around all day, focusing on our breath and being present. So while meditation is a good thing to do, it's also helpful to have other practices that remind us to be aware and present—something that doesn't require special situations or circumstances and ideally fits into an already established pattern in our lives. Like making dinner.

A Bowl of Lemons

WHEN I imagine a life without a bowl of lemons, the picture is sad and roughly textured, like burlap or the old crumbly grout that surrounds my kitchen sink that I've been meaning to replace for years now. Lemons offer so much and require so very little, except maybe a few pennies counted out at the market, or the effort of plucking one from your backyard tree if you happen to be so lucky. A single lemon is a nice thing, it's true, but a bowlful of lemons can offer you the world.

I advise keeping a few lemons around at all times, if possible—filling an attractive bowl and setting it on your kitchen table or counter would be perfect. No need to refrigerate them as they'll last a long while if you're diligent to use the ripest first and remove the occasional moldy specimen. Or if you find that doesn't work in your kitchen, refrigerate most of them but keep a small clutch—maybe three—on a plate on your counter. Just to see them, just to pass by them as you go throughout your day, can bring a smile and a twinkle of pleasure.

And while these moments of pleasure are far from inconsequential, there are endless, practical reasons for doing this as well.

In the sweet realm, lemons offer the possibility of lemon curd, lemonade, the necessary introduction of a tart note to balance a batch of strawberry jam. They can be coaxed into many types of pie, including the famous lemon meringue and Shaker lemon. Lemon cake: chiffon, pound, layer. Lemon puddings of all sorts, and mousses, and cold things like ice cream or sorbet. Lemon bars!

In the savory realm, there are few things that don't benefit from a final squeeze of lemon that will adjust the flavors with a quick, puckery hit of acid. There's also Moroccan salted lemons, lemon vinaigrette, lemon chicken, the delicious homemade condiment called gremolata, and any number of fish recipes. Risottos, pastas, flatbreads. And, of course, a quick squeeze of lemon can uplift a cup of tea or transform a mug of hot water for your morning tea meditation.

Both of these lists are woefully incomplete, of course, but the point, I hope, is taken. A bowl of lemons on your kitchen table is life-changing. It's essential. It's what good cooks, the best and most happiest cooks, do.

Lemon Curd
Makes about 2 cups

Keeping a jar of lemon curd in your refrigerator means that you will never be short on having something delightful and sweet in the house. It means you can ask someone over for an impromptu cup of tea, or make a simple dessert by layering it with Greek yogurt in pretty glasses for parfaits. Lemon curd can be spread on scones, biscuits, and those thin Danish cookies, especially the lemon ones for a double lemony punch. It works beautifully as a filling for tarts and cakes and can be stirred into whipped cream in dramatic swirls to top fresh fruit or folded into slightly softened vanilla ice cream.

Need more ideas? Use it on top of pancakes or as a filling for crepes or French toast. Make lemon mousse by gently but thoroughly folding it into whipped cream. The sweet/tartness of the lemons and the rich, creamy texture lends a note of sophistication but don't let that stop you from joining me in my favorite way to eat lemon curd: stealing a luscious spoonful (or two!) straight from the jar.

3 to 4 lemons

¾ cup sugar

1 stick cold unsalted butter, cut into pieces

5 large egg yolks

¼ teaspoon salt

PEEL three of the lemons, removing as little of the bitter white pith as possible. Set the peels aside. Cut the lemons in half and squeeze enough juice to measure ½ cup. Use the fourth lemon, if needed.

ADD the sugar and lemon peels to the bowl of a food processor and blend until the peels and sugar are ground very fine, about 30 seconds. Then add the butter, egg yolks, lemon juice, and salt to the bowl. Blend for about 15 seconds to incorporate everything. It's fine if the mixture looks curdled.

POUR the mixture into a small saucepan and place over very low heat. Cook until the mixture begins to thicken, 12 to 15 minutes, stirring constantly. A heatproof spatula comes in handy here, or a wooden spoon. Stay close and keep an eye on things, as it is very easy to overcook the mixture at this point, which will cause it to curdle. Don't let it come to a hard boil; if it does, remove the saucepan from the heat, continue to stir constantly until it settles down, and then return it to the heat.

TEST the curd for doneness by dipping a spoon into the curd. It should coat the spoon and when you run your finger through it, it should leave a clear, distinct path. The curd will continue to thicken as it cooks, so don't worry if it looks a little runny at this point. Remove from the heat.

PLACE a strainer over a bowl and pour the curd through it to catch any peel or coagulated egg. Pour the curd into a clean jar and allow it to cool to room temperature. (Or, if it fits, just place the sieve over the storage jar and strain it directly into it.) Seal the jar and store in your refrigerator where it will keep for several weeks. Unless, of course, you're like me and you eat it all up in a few days!

Note: If you don't have a food processor, you can remove the lemon peel with a zester or rasp and mix all the ingredients into a bowl by hand. In fact, I often find a rasp or microplane is the easiest way to remove lemon peel even if I am using the food processor.

Don't Wait

IN my pantry right now, there among the cans of tomato paste and chicken noodle soup, is a box of rich, decadent sipping chocolate, a bag of dried porcini, and a little tin of handmade candied violets. In my closet, a pair of fancy velvet heels and a gorgeous cashmere sweater mingle with the cotton shirts and clogs. Tucked away in a drawer, a small vial of a favorite, very expensive perfume waits for the special day that I will dab it on my wrists. Besides being wonderful and special, all these things have one other thing in common: I never use them. And I've been thinking that this has to change.

I have this habit of saving (hoarding perhaps?) certain things, special things, delicious things, things that normally don't appear in my everyday life. Why? Well, on the surface it seems logical. Because I may never have the chance to see them or taste them again, I become very careful with them and dole out their specialness in small, cautious doses. These resources are limited, after all, so they must be saved for a special day. Right? Well, maybe not.

Lately, I've been questioning this thinking. Is there something more going on here, some basic assumptions I am making about my life, about the world I live in? Is it really true that wonderful things are rare and limited and should be guarded? Is it really true that some days are more special than others? And the answer, while a bit more complicated than this, basically boils down to "no."

If I look really closely, I see this attitude originates in a sense of scarcity, a fundamental feeling that there's not enough. And not only that, this sense of scarcity is a habit, a basic, foundational attitude that permeates all aspects of my life. I don't lead with it but if I'm quiet and ask myself the right questions, I can see it there, lurking and influencing many of my thoughts and decisions.

And it persists even in the face of good evidence that actually I live in a time of enormous abundance. Everywhere I look, there is much to be grateful for, much to be appreciated. From the tumbled, tangled profusion of my pantry shelves to the way the sun is shifting into its spring position and spilling light through my kitchen window. The smile from a stranger passing on the sidewalk, the enormous selection of teas in my grocery store aisles, the presence of my friends and family, their wisdom and caring. This is the good life! This is cause for celebration!

Instead of saving the good stuff for later, what about throwing a party every day? What about splashing on that special perfume until the vial is empty and snuggling into that cashmere sweater before sitting down at my computer to work? And what about those delicious things in the pantry? What if I don't taste some sipping chocolate now and I get run over by a bus this afternoon? I will never, ever have had the chance to taste it, to enjoy its velvety texture and dark, nuanced bitterness. Is that how I want to live this life?

Of course, there are special things to mark special occasions. If we eat caviar every day, then it will eventually become just another boring spoonful of salty fish eggs. But at the same time, hoarding away the good stuff for a day that is more special than this day, right here and now, is also a mistake. In my life at least, there needs to be a balance, there needs to be more revelry, more recklessness.

So I've vowed to loosen it up a little. Every day, in small ways, I will stop what I'm doing and make a celebration. Maybe it will be pausing for a cup of hot sipping chocolate, or to splash on some perfume. Maybe I will add those porcini to my everyday lunch soup, or finally open that very nice bottle of wine before it turns to vinegar and invite a few friends over on a Wednesday night.

Whatever the circumstance, my new phrase is "don't wait." Don't wait for a day or a situation to be better, more special, more worthy of celebration, than this day, this moment. Right here, right now. Don't wait. Celebrate!

On Being Intimate
with Everything

ANOTHER way to look at being present is to think of it as being intimate. With everything. When we cook, one of the ways we are *intimate* is with the tangible world: with our bodies and our senses and the ingredients we are working with and the place where we are working. From the bits of bread dough underneath our fingernails to the pull on our muscles when we lift a heavy pot to the gentle squeeze we give a pear to see if it is ripe, cooking presents us with unlimited opportunities to experience an immediate sense of presence.

The primary path for this intimacy is through our senses and perceptions. We spend a lot of time ignoring much of what comes in through our senses, for the world is a big, noisy, complicated place and we need to filter out most of it in order to stay focused. Often this ignoring becomes a habit so that even when it's not too much, even when our immediate surroundings are quiet and safe, we are still a bit shut down and numbed out.

When we fully use and engage our senses, we begin

to develop or rediscover that we can trust what our bodies are telling us about the world around us. This allows us to open up more, to become more available to our experiences, and, in doing so, we learn to rely on this simple but powerful intelligence. For many of us, there's not much in our everyday lives that asks for this kind of engagement, so finding those moments where it is possible to drop in more deeply through our sense doors is both precious and necessary.

And, of course, cooking and being in the kitchen is overrun with these opportunities. We are exposed to endless opportunities for beauty and sensual pleasures, from the scent of thyme and garlic cooking in butter to the way it feels to thinly slice a zucchini into silky ribbons. Melting chocolate in heavy cream, running our hands through a sack of dried beans, plucking herbs from their woody stems—all these activities have the potential to awaken our senses. For some of us, this can also include hacking a knife through the joint of a chicken or stuffing a whole fish with thick slices of lemon and handfuls of fresh oregano.

It's an interesting experiment to see what happens when we do allow our senses to awaken, especially in a relatively safe and neutral and often deliciously sensual place like the kitchen. The process is simple. The next time you're engaged in a kitchen task, be it bruising a handful of basil leaves for pesto or chopping onions (if they're not too old and sulfurous and are causing tears) or stirring the polenta on a chilly winter's day, or slicing up some lemons, try to narrow your focus to just that task. To do this, look for physical sensations like the fragrance of the lemon or the sting of its juice on a torn cuticle or the slight resistance of your knife as you slice through—skin, flesh, seed. Listen for the sounds of the knife on the cutting board or the pounding of the mortar and pestle; watch for the subtle changes in the scent of onions when they move from raw to wilted to browned; notice the resistance of the polenta as it cooks and thickens, listen for how it sounds when it plops and burbles in the pot. Feel the weight of your body, the tension in your shoulders, the rush of saliva to your mouth when you smell something enticing.

Of course, your mind will wander but gently pull it back with the promise and the delight of your present activities. Give it your full attention and welcome it into the weave of your experience. Whenever I do this, I am sometimes surprised to experience a ping of joy—or if that's too much, then at least a sense of appreciation, which is necessary for joy. This feeling is important because we want to spend time with and return to the things that bring us pleasure.

On Loving Your Kitchen

HAVING a kitchen that functions well and is pleasing to be in is an important part of an intimate kitchen experience. Some of us have the good fortune to remake our kitchens into exactly what we want and others of us have to make do with our landlord's choices, but whatever the case, it's important to have positive feelings associated with being there. After all, it's very hard to be intimate with something that causes distress or discomfort as we naturally tend to avoid the things that make us unhappy. Our kitchens need to be a place we want to be in.

Sometimes, this can be as simple as the fact that your kitchen is the warmest place in a cold house on a winter afternoon. Or maybe you just purchased a set of canisters that you really love, and every time you walk in the room, you see them and they make you smile. Maybe it's the only room that captures the morning sun or most deeply expresses who you are. This is not about the perfect designer kitchen or the shiniest, newest appliances. This isn't about what money and an interior decorator can accomplish. This is about creating the best space you can, whether you own or rent or purchased your kitchen table at the local church thrift sale.

So attend to your kitchen. Cleanliness is an obvious component of this, but being sure your work surfaces are clutter-free and available is important, too. Organize your kitchen in a way that makes sense to you. Notice what brings you difficulty and try to solve that. If you bake a lot, then it might be worth it to purchase more than one set of measuring cups, for instance, so that you will always have a clean one available in the size you need. Or paint those cabinets white if your kitchen always feels too gloomy. There's no reason not to hang art in your kitchen (and it doesn't have to only be images of teapots and fruit bowls). If there's room, a comfortable chair for relaxing with a cup of coffee is a small but attainable luxury.

Some people create well in simple environments and others need more chaos to bring forth the muse. Don't judge your space by others' aesthetic notions and don't apologize for who you are. Instead, spend that energy on expressing and creating something delicious to nourish yourself or those you care for. Be unabashedly yourself. You can't do otherwise.

Broken

THE other day I dropped a favorite platter and it shattered with a rather alarming, dramatic crash. The expletive that quickly followed was equally loud and dramatic. A minute later, a neighbor gently knocked at my door to see if I was okay (sound carries easily in my apartment building, especially with springtime-opened windows). And I was okay, except for the embarrassment and sadness and frustration I was feeling. I had to wonder to myself: all this drama for a platter?

There is a famous Buddhist teaching about seeing a teacup as already broken. Even though it currently could be intact and firmly in our hands, the truth is the cup we are holding is bound to break one day, or get lost, or even stop being a favorite. So that event, that breaking or losing, is inherent in the cup and in our relationship to the cup. This is true, actually, of all things in life and the world, since nothing is permanent.

This feeling of impermanence can lead us in two opposite directions. One is attachment, obsession, fear: This is precious, I must cling to it and protect it. The other is carelessness and indifference: If it is already broken, already lost to me, then what's the use of caring?

So what to do? How to care about something on one hand and be completely free from attachment to it on the other? Tricky business but not without a solution, another way of being: appreciation. Knowing that something is already broken can give rise to appreciating it here in the moment, just as it is.

And letting it shatter when it's time for that, too. When something has been deeply appreciated, it's ironically a little easier to let it go and feel all the things that shattering brings: sadness, regret, nostalgia, even more appreciation.

So in sweeping up my favorite broken platter, I allowed myself to start missing it, to remember how much I enjoyed it, how I used it to serve up polenta with ragù in the winter and big, scattered salads in the summer. I remembered the person who gave it to me and the many kitchens and dining tables it had graced. And then I carefully emptied the dustpan full of broken, jagged pieces into a brown paper bag and carried it outside to the garbage bin. Thank you very much, favorite platter, and so long.

Soji (or How to Clean Everything)

IN many Zen temples, there's an activity called *soji*, a period of about 20 minutes where the whole community participates in cleaning up the temple and its grounds. It usually happens right after a bowing and chanting service, marking the end of the morning meditation schedule.

The premise is simple. You are assigned a simple cleaning task (rake the path, dry the dishes, sweep the hallway), which you do silently and without ambition to finish. In other words, there's no ownership of the task: Just pick up the broom and do the best job you possibly can sweeping the hall until it's time to stop. After about 20 minutes, the work leader walks around ringing a bell that signals the end of *soji*. When you hear the bell, you simply stop what you are doing. If the hallway is only half swept, if there are still dishes to be dried, if you only polished 12 of the 15 windowpanes—it doesn't matter. Just put away your tools and move on to the next thing. (In the case with most temples, this would be breakfast!)

Soji is a spiritual practice, an extension of meditation, where the fluid, open sensibility that was cultivated on the meditation cushion is brought to the task at hand. If we've had an experience of softening or opening up or had some kind of realization while sitting on the cushion but we cannot experience or manifest it while we're off the cushion, then that experience is not quite complete. We haven't finished fully integrating it. *Soji* gives us a chance to do the work of bringing meditation to our whole self and to notice in a very real way how well that's going.

So consider approaching some of the tasks in your life from the *soji* perspective. What would happen if it wasn't so much about finishing but more about simply doing? What burdens can be put down when we redirect our energies not toward the goal but into the process itself, into each moment along the way? What treasures are waiting for us there?

———·—·—·———

Another thing that *soji* teaches us is how to get tasks done even when we don't feel like doing them. The custom for *soji* is to receive and accept your work assignment without comment. It doesn't matter if you don't feel like drying the dishes or if you hate the smell of window cleaner or if you actually love turning the compost, for that matter. You just do what is assigned to you, in silence, and ideally with no preference. Or if you do have a preference, you learn to ignore it.

For this reason, I've found that "doing *soji*" is a great way to tackle unwelcome tasks in the home environment, too. Sometimes, a task is unwelcome because it is very big, or it involves something we're not skilled at, or requires too many decisions. Sometimes, it's just repetitive and boring and will need to be done again next week, or even later that day. Whatever it is, you can probably handle doing it for 20 minutes.

So the next time you find yourself resisting a kitchen task that really needs to get done, take the *soji* approach. Set a timer and make a vow that you will stay with it until the bell rings, and when it does, simply stop what you are doing. If you finish before the bell has rung, see if there isn't a smaller task you can pick up for a while— there is always something that needs tending, mending, prepping, or putting away in our lives. If it's a large task, find a smaller aspect of it that you can pick up and complete. Get some onions chopped for the big pot of soup you want to tackle later, measure out the ingredients and prep the pan for a cake, clean and sort one shelf in your pantry.

Or you can just build *soji* into your morning routine to stay on top of daily home maintenance or to do a little kitchen prep so that making dinner later that evening isn't such a burden. I have a friend who does this with her whole family before they leave the house each weekday morning (it's more like 5 minutes but five people doing *soji* for 5 minutes means a lot can get done!).

Framing your activity as *soji*, limiting the time, and then forgetting about the time as you plunge into the activity is not just a fantastic way to get things done, it's also a way to be present for all the moments in your life.

Occasionally Unplugged

THERE'S nothing wrong with owning a collection of bright, shiny small appliances, unless of course they sit neglected, taking up precious shelf space and growing a layer of dust. Tools are useful and if having a food processor at the ready makes all the difference between turning that patch of garden basil into pesto or letting it go to seed, then far be it from me to object. My own food processor may be an old and faded white plastic model from the early 1980s but it occupies a prime spot in my kitchen for reasons more practical than aesthetic: It still works like a charm (or more accurately, like a charming workhorse), and I use it frequently.

And yet there is something to be said for going unplugged every now and then, for pulling down a mortar and pestle or grabbing a large bowl and a wooden spoon and working up a light sweat. There's an honesty in the labor, a certain kind of fulfillment that comes when you've done something a little more strenuous than press a button. Unplugged preparation allows the opportunity for all the senses to fully be a part of the experience: the smells, the sounds, the way it feels when a vinaigrette begins to thicken and emulsify. Without the intermediary of a machine, we notice subtle changes in scent and texture and can easily dip a tip of a finger into whatever we are working on for a quick taste.

It's rare for us to have an experience these days unmediated by machinery of some sort so it can be a little thrilling to create something simply from a handful of ingredients and our own bodies. Besides, going unplugged is fun. Maybe you've had a bit of a day and the notion of pounding the hell out of a clove of garlic and a bunch of innocent herbs is an appealing, cathartic experience.

So if time and energy allow, try going unplugged in your kitchen every now and then. Make your next batch of pesto with a mortar and pestle or use it to crush the spices for your curry instead of the mini coffee grinder. Beat the butter and sugar by hand until fluffy when making a cake, whip cream with a hand whisk, make your coffee in a French press. Why? For the simple reason that you may discover that what you lose in efficiency is more than made up for in the satisfaction and pleasure of giving something 100 percent of your whole, wonderful self.

A Simple Weeknight Curry
Serves 4 to 6

—●—

This is one of my favorite throw-together
weeknight meals, as many of the ingredients come
from canned goods that I regularly keep in my
pantry. It is infinitely versatile. If you don't have
cauliflower or carrots, for instance, feel free to sub in
what you do have on hand: green beans, cubed
squash, broccoli. A handful of frozen peas thrown in
during the final 5 minutes would be good, too.
Do try to keep the potatoes, though, as their
starch helps to thicken the sauce.

I learned to make this curry with that classic
turmeric-yellow curry powder found in most grocery
stores and so have a nostalgic allegiance to its flavor
and convenience. That said, if you have a favorite,
from-scratch curry blend of your own, feel free
to use it here. I'm sure it will shine.

1 clove garlic

½ teaspoon peppercorns

½ teaspoon coriander seeds

2 tablespoons oil such as canola or grapeseed

1 tablespoon curry powder

1 (28-ounce) can chopped tomatoes

2 cups sliced potatoes

2 cups sliced carrots

2 cups cauliflower florets

1 (14-ounce) can coconut milk

1 (14-ounce) can chickpeas, drained

2 tablespoons soy sauce, plus more if needed

1 tablespoon fish sauce

1 tablespoon honey, plus more if needed

Hot chile paste (optional)

¼ cup slivered basil leaves, plus small whole
leaves for garnish

Cooked rice, for serving

IN a mortar, grind the garlic, peppercorns, and coriander seeds into a paste. (Alternatively, finely chop the garlic with already ground versions of the peppercorns and coriander to make the paste.)

HEAT the oil in a Dutch oven. Fry the garlic mixture until fragrant, about 1 minute. Add the curry powder and fry a little longer to release the flavors.

ADD the tomatoes (with juice), potatoes, and carrots and bring to a gentle simmer, adding a splash of water if there isn't enough liquid. After about 5 minutes, add the cauliflower, coconut milk, chickpeas, soy sauce, fish sauce, and honey. Bring to a gentle simmer and continue cooking until the vegetables are done and the sauce has begun to thicken.

TASTE for seasonings and add additional soy sauce or honey, as needed. You may want to add more heat via hot chile paste if your curry powder wasn't hot enough.

REMOVE from the heat and stir in the basil. Serve over rice with the additional basil on top as a garnish.

Variations:

Add cubes of cooked chicken or raw shrimp toward the end of the final simmer and cook until done.

For a vegan version, use a vegan fish sauce or more soy sauce, and substitute agave for the honey.

If you want to keep things supereasy, skip the rice and serve with store-bought naan or flatbreads, toasted on the stovetop until slightly charred and hot.

Extra-fancy step: Serve with bowls of plain yogurt or raita, toasted coconut, roasted cashews, coarsely chopped cilantro, chutney, and other simple garnishes.

The Perfect Pot

CONFESSION: I am not immune to the allure of a sleek, sexy, multi-ply, copper-clad saucier pan. I, too, sigh with longing at those gorgeous European stoves and handsome, handmade mortar and pestles that are the size of my kitchen sink. I completely get it that kitchen stuff is an easy addiction, that it is possible to tumble into excess when it comes to handmade plates and vintage napkins and enameled ladles from Great Britain. I am absolutely the last person to preach austerity and restraint when it comes to outfitting my favorite room in the house.

But I'm also not a fan of stuffing my kitchen full of unused and useless equipment that does nothing but collect dust and take up space. Over the years, I have developed a simple rule that allows me to acquire what I need for my kitchen without going overboard. Whether it's an item that I pick up every day or only once a year, it all boils down to one question: Does this make me happy? What that means to me is that it has to perform the task it was built for with integrity and relative ease, and ideally it should be beautiful. Not pretty, but beautiful, in the way that things are beautiful even if they are stained and battered, even if someone else would laugh at its color or trade it in for a newer model. In other words, I have to love it. Not because it is the latest or the most expensive or most trendy, but because it feels good when I pick it up.

One of my favorite kitchen pieces is a small enameled lid I purchased in San Francisco's Chinatown years and years ago. It has a jaunty little knob on top and a few abstract flowers airbrushed here and there. It fits on all of my smaller frying pans, which did not come with lids of their own. I think it cost all of 49 cents.

I also treasure a large red Le Creuset Dutch oven that was a gift from my mother. I remember opening it one Christmas morning and saying to myself, "This is something that I will keep forever." And I have. I feel this way about my knives, which I have collected over the years: Some are fancy, some very humble, but all are a joy to pick up. There's also a favorite bean pot, made of red clay that was polished until it turned black, and the prettiest old linen dish towel, with bright yellow, red, green, and blue stripes, found at a thrift store in San Francisco's Mission district. I'm not sure why this is, but every time I pick up that towel, I smile a little.

So seek out kitchen equipment that you enjoy using. Select pots and pans that you find easy to lift and knives and cooking spoons that feel good in your hands. Purchase the highest quality you can afford (but don't be fooled into thinking that high prices are always the best), and take good care of it for life. The best frying pan, the most perfect pot, is the one that you want to use. It's the one that makes you happy when you pull it from the cupboard. Everything else just gets in the way.

Posture

HOW we carry and support our bodies in the kitchen will determine our strength, endurance, and overall happiness. Posture is important because it is the center and the framework from which all movement and gesture originates. It's what holds us up.

Paying attention to our posture is a way to focus our awareness and to practice presence. Posture is an indication of who we are in a particular moment, what we are feeling, and how we are coping. When we are droopy or hunched over, it's an indication that perhaps we need to rest or stretch or to sit down to chop those carrots. When we are upright and supported, we can carry on with the task at hand, offering it our energy and ability, simultaneously holding and being held by our efforts.

Our posture is also echoed in our thoughts. There is a posture of the mind as well as the body, a basic open and aware stance that we can cultivate in order to encourage a more balanced and receptive mind. When we are upright in all aspects of our lives, we create a core stability from which we can draw, like a deer drinking deeply from a pond in the middle of a forest.

———.———.———

Since cooking is work, often hard physical work, it's good to check in with your body now and then to be sure things are still loose and flowing nicely. It's easy to get hunched up while powering through a pile of onions or to wrench your back while carrying a heavy pot of water. One part of your body that can take the most beating in the kitchen is your feet. Restaurant workers, along with nurses, physicians, and other people who are on their feet all day, long ago eschewed fashion in favor of the clunky but practical clogs, which look funny at first until you realize that they are helping your feet every single minute of every single day.

So whenever I'm going to tackle a long, complicated recipe that involves a lot of standing and chopping and stirring and cleaning up, I take a cue from the professionals and don my kitchen clogs (which also happen to be close-toed, another professional kitchen footwear tip). Confession: I've been known to wear my clogs outside of the kitchen as well because they're just that great, and let's face it, once you understand that you don't have to distort and stuff your feet into uncomfortable shoes in order to live a happy life, you will never turn back.

———·——·——·———

So remember to check in with your posture and your body while working in the kitchen. Let it tell you something about how you are doing or feeling so you can respond appropriately. There's wisdom in knowing when to put down your knife and simply stretch your arms over your head or when to sit down for a spell to shell the beans. Pay close attention and listen. Be a good friend to yourself.

How a Bowl of Bread Dough Can Teach Us the Way to Live

THE other day it occurred to me that all the delicious things in life—bread, cheese, wine, beer, pickles, kraut, just-cooked meats—become more delicious because of rest, because built into their process is a time where they sit quietly and do nothing. Actually, that's not quite true. They are doing something: Yeasts are eating sugars and burping carbon dioxide, juices are being absorbed, fermentation is being initiated, and so on. But from the point of view of the cook, we are leaving it alone. We are taking our hands off of the process and allowing the wild and uncontrolled elements to take their turn.

What would happen if we did the same thing for ourselves in our own lives?

Everyone knows soups and stews taste better after they've spent a day in the fridge. Fruit is astonishing in its flavor and sweetness when it's allowed to ripen to its absolute fullest. Vinegars, cured meats like ham and sausage, cured fish, salted lemons, soy and fish sauces—

all our favorite foods benefit from some quiet time, from a period of rest.

All this leads me to thinking about people and how we seldom give ourselves resting time. It can be a little alarming, this pace at which we are living our lives. How often do we allow ourselves to rest, to just stop? We chase about here and there, tense, worried, full of stress, too busy to notice what's happening around us as we whiz through the scenery, on to the next thing before we're even through with what's in front of us. How can we absorb and process our experiences when we've barely had time to register them?

And even when it is possible, many of us find it hard to stop. Maybe this is because to some degree, our self-worth and identity have become defined by our busy-ness. Who would we be if we weren't so busy? What would happen if we were to slow down some?

The bowl of bread dough, the cheese, the bottle of wine teach us that so much magic happens when we stop and rest. Flavor and depth develop, texture, medicine, nuance, transformation. For people, this is the time when we integrate all the experiences, all the input we've taken in throughout the day. Rest is the time when we sift through and digest and transform. This isn't about sleep. This is about sitting still for a while, alert but quiet, allowing an internal process to take over, allowing something that's not a product of our thinking and our actions to have influence.

When we stop our busyness, we settle more into our experiences, into our own skin. What does that feel like? Is it uncomfortable? Is it delightful? Strange? Familiar? Resting is a time to tune in, to reflect, to fully own and live in our lives. This is where we can ferment, transform, cure. This is where the magic happens.

Resting can be a period of meditation, or 15 minutes spent gazing out the window of your commuter train or bus. It can be lying flat on your back in the grass and watching the clouds or the stars. Swing low in a hammock, sip a cup or glass of something while sitting in a chair, stretch out on the floor and watch the dust filter through a sunbeam. Rest is available to us everywhere. Where will you find it?

Try it. Just stop. Just rest. Let the magic happen.

Patience

THE kitchen is a great teacher, and one of the greatest lessons it can teach us is patience, for some things simply cannot be rushed. If the bread is baked before it has risen properly, if the tomatoes are added to the pan before the onions have had a chance to soften, if the chicken is removed from the oven before it has cooked all the way to the bone, the final results will be lackluster at best and inedible and a waste of time and precious resources at worst.

So within its most basic definition—accepting or tolerating a delay—patience is a fundamental kitchen skill: Sometimes (often), we simply need to wait. Are there good but impatient cooks? Probably a few. But there are far, far more great, if not extraordinary, cooks who understand and practice the fine art of patience. They not only merely accept or tolerate delay but actually welcome it as a necessary part of a process.

In the kitchen, patience is as essential as a good, sharp knife. Some people might argue that cooking is about bashing about our ingredients so that they do our will. After all, we beat, pound, knead, thwack, pulverize, and chop all manner of things when cooking. But a good cook knows that cooking is less about bashing and more about listening and responding. We work with raw materials, with agricultural products that have natural seasons, and thus we are tasked with the proposition of working with constant change and inconsistency. Taste, texture, sweetness, and size are always shifting, and a good cook has to understand this and adjust accordingly. She has to have patience with what is before her so she can coax out its most delicious flavors.

Patience and intimacy and acceptance allow the things and circumstances and people in our lives to come forward and be just as they are. This, of course, doesn't mean we won't seek to change them. The whole carrot needs to be chopped, injustice needs to be challenged, an unhelpful habit needs to be curbed. But first, before we act, we need to fully understand what we are changing because we need to do more than dismantle something, we need to understand just what it wants to become next. Patience allows for this. In fact, it is necessary.

It is often wrongly assumed that patience is a passive stance, that the acceptance needed to work with patience creates a powerlessness. But the truth is, patience flows from a place of strength and wisdom. Patience allows for whatever we are working with to come forward and tell us what it needs, what it can ultimately become. It helps us to collaborate, not dominate, in our interactions with the world. Patience creates a pause and, therefore, an opportunity to respond from something deeper than our own habits and neuroses.

There's no doubt that our time in the kitchen will give us plenty of opportunity to practice patience so remember to approach it exactly as that: a practice—an ongoing, dynamic, open relationship with the uncontrollable, impermanent world. Impatience, irritability, frustration are indications that we're not satisfied with, not aligned with, our current circumstances. How do we respond? Should we give things a little shove in the right direction or should we allow the scene to play out on its own? Which is the better response? What is the most helpful thing in that moment? Step back for a few seconds and practice patience, and the answer will come.

Beyond the Five Senses

WE all know about our five basic senses: sight, sound, taste, touch, and smell. It's not hard to imagine how these are all brought into use when we cook. But it turns out some scientists believe that we possess much more than our five basic senses or, perhaps more specifically, that our five senses are only broad categories for a more complex array of sensory input.

For instance, we have a sense called proprioception that allows us to know where parts of our bodies are in relationship to other parts so we can do things like reach down and scratch our leg without having to look at our leg first. There's equilibrioception, which gives us a sense of balance and gravity and what direction is up or down. Thirst and hunger are also considered to be senses as well as our ability to sense how much time as passed.

Our sense of taste is complicated, too, with each aspect a distinct event: salty, sweet, bitter, sour, and savory. (Some people even speculate that fat is a taste as well.) Our sense of touch includes the ability to detect heat and cold, pleasure and pain, texture, and pressure.

When we cook, we engage all of our senses, from the basic to the more complex. Because of this, cooking offers us a capacity for deep pleasure and connection. Try it sometime: If you find that you're feeling blue or disconnected or out of sorts, reach for a not-too-hard but not-too-easy recipe. Maybe something that calls for wonderful smelling spices and a certain amount of chopping, like a stew or a curry. What happens when you allow the moment, which is full of sensory pleasure, to come forward? What happens when you untangle yourself from your habitual thinking and just respond to what your many senses are allowing in, the vast and complex mix of smells and tastes and sensations? Let it all in, with your feet firmly on the ground and your heart resting in the warm, sweet, savory, textured pleasure of being alive.

———•—•—•—

An experienced cook can lift her head up from chopping a carrot, sniff the air, and declare that the chicken roasting in the oven is ready just by the scent alone. A backup timer may be set for the recipe's suggested cooking time but cooking is rarely an exact science, and knowing when something is done, or nearing that narrow window of doneness, by smell or touch (and of course taste) is actually a more reliable tool. Even the sounds of cooking can carry clues. Jam, for instance, moves from a light bubbly sound to a slower, heavier *plop* as it thickens.

Newer cooks can learn this seemingly magical ability by remaining alert and present and filing away sensory clues, which isn't difficult to do but sometimes difficult to remember to do. This is why awareness is so important in the kitchen and why cooking while distracted is possible (somewhat) but seldom desirable. The beauty about learning how to cook is that the wait time between opportunities to put what we've learned into practice is very short. Every scent, every burble, every change in texture is an opportunity to learn and grow and become a more experienced, more relaxed, more engaged cook.

As with anything new, time and practice will bring more ease, and more ease allows a greater capacity to absorb experience. When we're fretting and full of anxiety, as we often are when we're first learning something, it's all we can do to get through the task. But still, those sensory clues are always there—available, reliable, and usually quite pleasant to experience. In time, they will be your most valued kitchen tool.

A Radical Suggestion

ONE way to become a better cook is to experiment with not using a kitchen timer. I know! This sounds like absolute madness—a certain disaster in the making! Or at the very least an invitation to a more fretful and anxious kitchen experience. Maybe so, but stay with me here.

First, let's be clear: Kitchen timers are very handy tools, and I'm by no means suggesting we should do away with them completely. They have an important place in our kitchens and have no doubt prevented innumerable culinary catastrophes the world over. So the idea here isn't to toss our timers out completely. But we can try to become less reliant on them.

Why? To begin with, our kitchens and the equipment in them can vary significantly. Oven temperatures are notoriously inaccurate; pots and pans differ in size, material, and thickness. Ingredients, too, can vary from day to day: thicker, juicier, bigger, smaller. Because of this, relying on the cooking time given in a recipe can be risky, especially the first few times we make it. Just because a recipe says it will take 20 minutes doesn't necessarily mean it will, or it may take 20 minutes this week but 15 minutes the next time you make it.

But even more significantly, when we depend exclusively on a kitchen timer to tell us when something is done, we sacrifice a deeper level of attentiveness. We set the dial and then move on, often forgetting entirely about the thing we are cooking until we hear the bell. We're not checking in as much along the way, so we don't develop an understanding of how a dish evolves while cooking. We're not learning or exploring or training our senses.

Without a timer, we remain alert to what's cooking. Our senses are heightened, and we can feel a slight pull toward the stove. We stay in relationship to our dish, even when it has disappeared into the oven or beneath a lid. It's always in the back of our minds, a little tug that tells us not to forget. We sniff the air, we open the lid, we poke, we taste, we stay on it.

Of course, there are occasions when a timer should definitely be used, such as when you are cooking many different recipes at once or if it's a particularly distracted or stressed day. But occasionally forgoing a kitchen timer under more forgiving circumstances is an interesting and informative way to cook.

If you just can't see yourself not using a timer, take up the attitude that a timer is only a suggestion, a simple reminder that it's time to check on things. Set it a few minutes early so you can observe your dish as it's cooking and get a better sense of what it needs to look and smell and taste and sound like when it's done.

Sometimes, our most important task is to pay attention. When we bring attention to our cooking, when we bring all of our senses to bear and remain engaged with the process at all steps, chances are something delicious will follow. But even if we fail and produce something inedible, if we were paying attention, we will have learned something useful from that failure.

The poet Mary Oliver says that attention is the beginning of devotion. What consumes your attention and is it worthy of it? What are you devoted to today?

Almost-Any-Fruit Custard Tart
Makes an 11-inch tart, enough for 8 to 12 people

———

This is an absolutely favorite tart, one that I have been making for my entire adult life. People always want the recipe, and I am always happy to share, which is why it is here. What's great about this tart is that the custard is unsweetened, meaning that all the sweetness comes from the crust and the fruit, leaving the custard to be a lovely, savory, silky contrast. Since the crust contains all the sugar, it caramelizes when baked, creating a deep sweetness and a crisp, slightly chewy texture.

While many fruits will work in this tart, not all are suitable. It originally came to me as a cherry tart, using canned cherries that have been well drained of their juices. While this was delicious, I started making it with fresh cherries at some point and have gone on from there to experiment with many different kinds of fruit. I especially like figs (halved or quartered) and fresh apricots or plums (split in two, stoned, and arranged cut side down). Pears or apples are good but need to be cooked first. I peel and slice them, then sauté them in a small amount of butter until just heated through and beginning to soften before arranging them on the crust, usually in a spiral pattern.

Experiment with any fruit that captures your fancy but keep in mind that only fruit that takes well to cooking will work here. Steer clear of melons, for instance, and also any fruit that needs to have a lot of sugar added in order to be good, such as cranberries.

1¼ cups flour

½ teaspoon salt

½ teaspoon ground cinnamon (see Note on page 94)

½ teaspoon baking powder

1 stick unsalted butter, at room temperature

1 cup sugar

2 cups fresh fruit (see above)

2 eggs

2 cups half-and-half

PREHEAT the oven to 375°F.

IN a medium bowl, mix together the flour, salt, cinnamon, and baking powder and set aside.

USING an electric or stand mixer, cream the butter and sugar. Add the flour mixture and mix briefly, just to combine. The mixture should be crumbly but moist enough to hold together when pressed. Set aside ¼ cup.

Press the remaining dough into an 11-inch tart pan with removable bottom. Be sure to really press in the mixture and that the sides are built up high enough and thick enough to hold the custard.

ADD the fruit, spreading it evenly over the bottom of the tart. Sprinkle on the reserved ¼ cup of the flour mixture. Place the tart pan on a baking sheet (to catch any spills when you add the custard later) and slide it into the oven. Bake for 15 minutes, or until the shell has just started to turn golden. It will have puffed up slightly.

WHILE the shell is baking, whisk the eggs in a small bowl, then add the half-and-half and whisk until combined. After 15 minutes, open the oven door and pull the baking sheet (not the oven rack) partway out of the oven. Holding the baking sheet steady, carefully and quickly pour the custard mixture into the tart, filling as close to the top as you dare. Carefully push the baking sheet back in and close the oven door. Bake for another 25 minutes, or until the crust is deep golden brown and the custard is set.

REMOVE from the oven and let cool slightly before removing the outer tart ring. Let cool completely before sliding off the bottom. Serve at room temperature or slightly chilled. This tart is best eaten the day it is baked, as the crust can become soft over time.

Note: You may want to swap out the cinnamon for another ground spice, such as cardamom or maybe a combination of spices such as star anise and cinnamon and ginger—very good with pears!

Tending

THE dishes are washed, rinsed, and piled up to dry. The carrots and onions peeled, chopped, measured, cooked. The soup stirred and seasoned, tasted and seasoned again, and left on the back of the stove, barely simmering but not forgotten. The table wiped down, the floor swept, the groceries stowed in the cupboards. Dishcloths washed and folded and stacked and placed in the drawer, next to the clean and sorted silverware.

Stovetop splatters polished away, the garbage taken out, a chicken left to thaw in the refrigerator. Feeding the bread starter, lining up the dish soap and sponge on the edge of the sink, filling the kettle for tomorrow's first cup of tea. A clean cup on the countertop, waiting.

———·—·—·———

The kitchen is a place of tending, a place where we take care of things. When we tend to something, we create connection, and, over time, this connection deepens into intimacy. Intimacy is a basic human need but more than that, intimacy tempers our idea that there's not enough, it soothes our restless yearning and the fearful little whispers that make us lose track of what's most important. It fills in the cracks and mends the weak places and sands down the rough spots until they're smooth and pleasing to touch.

In the kitchen, we learn and practice and actualize these connections through taking care of small, simple things: filling the sugar bowl, mending a cracked plate, cleaning the meat from the leftover roast chicken for sandwiches and stock. We learn that we are always in relationship to something, be it the sinkful of spinach or another human being's desires or even our own restless thoughts. To be in relationship is to be vulnerable, and because vulnerability can sometimes be quite challenging for us, it helps to approach it all with a certain amount of tenderness, a gentle caring, a careful touch.

It's true that the kitchen can be a place for fierceness, too, and wild drama and toughness. This fierceness has its important contributions and lessons, and its own kind of connection and intimacy. If you've badly scalded your hand or had to fight a pest invasion, then you might know something of this.

But mostly, the kitchen is where we make the soup and fill the kettle and fold the towels. It's where we learn the lessons of feeding and being fed, how to give and receive, and to understand what is most precious and what it means to take care of that. This is what the kitchen can teach us, if only we would let it.

When You Wash the Dishes, the Dishes Also Wash You

THERE are some chores that we immediately dismiss with an automatic, unexamined sense of dislike. Consider the pile of unwashed dishes or the recipe that begins with the instructions to chop six onions or the weekly mopping up of the kitchen floor. Sheer drudgery, right? And yet, taking on these so-called boring chores can offer us much more than the small ping of satisfaction that comes when we complete them. Drudgery tasks are often very simple and so can be used as an opportunity to bring some sense of relaxation and presence. We can shed the extra armor and concerns that have built up over the day and invite into our lives a moment or two of quiet simplicity and reflection.

A kitchen chore will often tether us to a place: the sink, the chopping board, the stove. This is a good thing. On the surface, this tethering may feel like a restriction but it's actually really helpful to restrict our options sometimes. This is in part what seated meditation is all about: quieting the external distractions so we can turn our attention inward in order to see more clearly what is happening there. Standing at the stove or over a sinkful of dishes, it is possible to touch some of this stillness and insight while still in the midst of activity, especially if the task is simple or repetitive or one we know very well. Like chopping celery or stirring a sauce.

Think of this chore-doing as time for integration, where we can fold in the experiences of the day and assimilate the lessons learned—the mistakes, the triumphs, and all the mundane stuff, too. Taking time to allow the day to settle and register like this is a key component to a happy, richly experienced life. Rushing through a dreaded chore just to get it done is a missed opportunity; relaxing into the rhythms of simple work and allowing the body and spirit to align after a busy day is golden.

This is how when you wash the dishes, the dishes also wash you.

———•—•—•———

Even with the promise of reflection, alignment, and happiness, we still may find that we're reluctant to pick up a difficult or boring kitchen task. In these moments, I feel it's okay to use props and pleasures to lure us to the sink or stove. Playing music or listening to the radio or podcasts is certainly a popular chore enhancer. Investing in a piece of equipment that is a pleasure to use is another little trick: It can be something as simple as a delicious-smelling cleaning product. These small touches can be just enough to encourage us to sink more deeply into our everyday activities and help us to find relaxation and perhaps even a moment of pleasure there.

All You Need Is . . .

AS much as I wish it weren't the case, the difficult truth of it is that I'm a lousy gardener. I just don't have a good feel for plants and their needs. I get anxious and overwater, and then I get distracted and underwater. I overexpose some plants to the sun while at the same time underexposing others, all the while losing track of when they were last fed or sometimes even what kind of plant I am tending. Only the heartiest of plants (geraniums and rosemary) seem to be able to survive my efforts. This terrible affliction has one upside, though: It helps me to have empathy for those folks who are just like me, only it's the kitchen that flummoxes them. Not everyone has a natural talent for cooking.

There are two things (well, three actually, but more on that later) needed to remedy this so-called lack of talent: persistence and experience. Quite simply, if you're not good at cooking or some aspect of cooking, keep doing it until you are good enough. Take classes, talk to people, ask for help and instruction, read and research, and most important, get into the kitchen and keep at it. Over time, you will get better, and, eventually, you will develop what seemed elusive in the beginning: that instinct for what a dish needs, that intuition for when something is perfectly done, that ability to put together delicious and interesting ingredients with seemingly no effort at all.

The formula is simple. Begin with acquiring some basic knowledge and technique and follow it up with practice and persistence. Eventually, you will become experienced and that experience will help you relax enough so that you will develop a more instinctual approach to your cooking, what the French call *au pif*, meaning by the nose.

With a gardening failure, my turnaround time for investigating and learning from my mistakes is lengthy. When I accidentally kill off a tomato plant in July, I can't try growing tomatoes again until the following year. But in the kitchen, when we make mistakes and are on the steep edge of a learning curve, we can begin again the next day or even the next moment.

Meanwhile, don't be discouraged by the more experienced cook who wanders into the kitchen, takes a sip of the broth cooking away on the stove, casually adds a few grains of salt and a touch of lemon juice, and wanders out again leaving behind something infinitely more elevated and delicious. To a new cook, this may seem like she just waved a magic wand over the pot but those few gestures with the salt and lemon actually came from years of tasting broths, years of adding not enough salt, then too much salt until an instinct for what was needed emerged.

I'm a firm believer that this can happen for everyone.

The big question is: What keeps us going until we build enough experience to become more instinctual cooks? How can we stay with it through sad and flavorless broths and overdone roast chickens and limp, floppy salads? The answer is simple. Love. Love is the third and most important thing. Love will give you the energy, enthusiasm, connection, and perseverance to stay with it. Love will inspire you to want to cook delicious things for those you care about. Love will keep you at it even when your body and spirit are tired. Cultivate your heart, and don't be surprised when you find love showing up in all of your dishes, the secret/not-so-secret sauce that is more powerful than salt or lemon. Don't believe me? Think this is all wishy-washy nonsense? Check it out for yourself. Next time you're standing at the stove, stirring a sauce, put a little love into it and see what happens.

Staying Close to Difficulty

FOR all its coziness and warmth, the kitchen can also have a more rugged sensibility where we are exposed to less pleasant things like death, rot, or infestation. What happens to this sense of intimacy when we encounter soured milk or mold on our sandwich, or our own squeamishness around killing? What happens when we have a visceral moment of realizing that meat is the muscle or organs of a once-living thing or when we find that our sack of flour has been invaded by creepy-crawly critters?

The urge to pull away can be powerful and sometimes even necessary, for these encounters bring us close to or, in some cases, directly confronted with our own mortality. How we meet this, how we work with these more challenging aspects of cooking is equally as important and compelling as smelling the crushed basil in a sunbeam-filled kitchen. What do you find disturbing and why? Is aversion the only way to respond to difficulty? Is it possible to shift to a more neutral feeling or even toward curiosity?

The important thing is to notice when you are contracting away from something and, if possible, question it. The next time you are in the middle of pulling away from something that brings you distress, see if you can pause and stay present for a moment. You may continue to pull away or you may discover that whatever it is you're confronting isn't as bad or as horrifying as you thought.

And, of course, it's different for everyone. Some people make good butchers and others are better off growing pole beans and carrots. Some people relish the deep complexity of fermented fish sauce and others won't come within 10 feet of a wedge of blue cheese. Some find the sweet, soft squish of a pudding repellent and are only happy with sharp, robust flavors. There is no right or wrong here, only the act of noticing, only the request to allow your experience to bloom fully before you cut it off.

So yes, it's not always sunbeams and honey buckets in the kitchen. There are plenty of moments of difficulty, disaster, tedium, and anxiety. Practicing with displeasure, being present for the uncomfortable or painful, is a powerful kitchen teaching and one that cannot be ignored. But it's helpful to begin with the more pleasing things, especially if that's not something you find yourself usually doing. Become familiar with the act of noticing, receiving, accepting in the more easeful atmosphere of pleasure and enjoyment so that you have some ground, some internal muscle, for when life becomes more challenging, as it inevitably will.

Just Two Ingredients

Cooking doesn't have to be a long and complicated process. In fact, sometimes cooking isn't actually cooking, it's more of a gathering and assembling process, a quick and spontaneous pairing of two (or maybe three) delicious things.

These recipes are a lesson in how simplicity and restraint can create an almost magical, greater-than-the-sum-of-its-parts deliciousness. Here are a few suggestions for those times that you are very hungry and want something immediate and satisfying.

A SNACK FOR A HOT SUMMER AFTERNOON

PLACE a few big dollops of the best yogurt you can find into an attractive dish. Chop a sweet, ice-cold cucumber into smallish pieces and stir it into the yogurt. Eat slowly under the shade of a tree or sitting in front of a fan. Sweet version: Sub in homemade apricot or strawberry jam for the cucumber.

TOMATOES AND SALT

IF you happen to grow tomatoes in your garden, you may already know this one. If you don't have garden-grown tomatoes, beg, barter, or steal a beautiful, perfectly ripe specimen or at least use one you got from the farmers' market. This is not for supermarket tomatoes. (In fact, there are very few uses for supermarket tomatoes.)

SALT is the second ingredient. If you only have regular table salt, that will do but if you have some fancy, flaky salt, this is the time to bring it out. If you're feeling civilized, slice the tomato into thick slices, sprinkle with the salt, and eat at your table with a knife and fork, napkin in lap. If you're feeling hedonistic, simply bite into the whole tomato as if it were an apple, sprinkling on the salt as you go. This will be a delightfully messy business, preferably done outdoors and maybe even in the middle of your tomato patch. Food miles: zero. Pleasure: off the charts.

BREAD AND CHOCOLATE

CUT a somewhat thick slice from a good loaf of bread. A bread made with eggs, such as challah, is rich and refined but a nice, yeasty, rustic loaf is really wonderful, too. Take a bar of your favorite chocolate (dark chocolate or one of those not-so-sweet dark milk chocolates is best) and either grate it or chop it into small pieces with a large chef's knife on a chopping board. You want enough chocolate to form a ¼-inch layer on the bread. Pile the chocolate on the bread slice, leaving a small margin around the perimeter so the chocolate can spread a little as it melts.

PLACE the bread in a toaster oven and toast until the chocolate begins to melt. Watch carefully, as the chocolate can easily burn. Just keep it in there long enough to soften a little, not melt completely, preferably on a lower rack, if possible. Carefully remove from the oven and use a knife to spread the chocolate evenly over the bread. Then simply cut in half and enjoy. (Bonus: This is really good with a pinch of crunchy sea salt flakes sprinkled on top, but then that would make this three ingredients, so just pretend you didn't read this. Or use one of those fancy salted chocolate bars.)

OTHER POSSIBILITIES FOR TINY RECIPES

SLICES of crisp apple with an aged cheddar; a poached egg sprinkled with crunchy Maldon salt or served with a dollop of leftover salsa verde (page 199); hot Japanese rice rolled into shiso leaves; crisp radishes with salted goat butter; sweet melon served in wedges, sprinkled with a very finely sliced basil chiffonade; a whole date stuffed with an almond; a half of a very ripe peach, the pit removed and the little hollow stuffed with ricotta; fresh, very ripe figs split in half and drizzled with honey or, for a savory take, a dollop of goat cheese.

Listening to the Basil

I brought home a huge bunch of basil from the farmers' market the other day. Even in that open-air, cacophonous market atmosphere, the intense smell of this basil hit me from 6 feet away and stopped me in my tracks. Vigorous and spicy, its leaves were thick and hearty, almost leatherlike. This was field basil, grown in the intense heat of California's Capay Valley where it was pulled up by its roots, bound into large messy bunches, and stuffed into pails of water for market day. I wanted to bring home an armload but I stopped myself at just one bunch. It now sits in a vase in the middle of my kitchen table, its feisty presence a reminder of the intense, fleeting nature of life. *Pay attention!* it demands. And I do.

We can spend a lot of time on autopilot in the kitchen. This is especially true if we're somewhat experienced cooks and are chopping our thousandth onion or reaching for a pot that has hung in that same place on the wall for 14 years. Our muscle memory automatically takes over, and we can move freely, almost unthinkingly, in a space that's familiar. This can be a pleasant, in-the-zone feeling but it's easy to cross over into a kind of fog where the simultaneously sensuous and dangerous nature of the kitchen is dulled. We're buzzing around the kitchen, our minds somewhere else, and then suddenly we slip and cut ourselves, or forget to add the garlic, or miss the opportunity to add that inspirational handful of chopped basil.

So it helps to have something around to remind us to be awake, aware, and engaged with our surroundings. This is where my bunch of basil comes in. It reminds me to pay closer attention to the senses that are usually more in the background, such as smell or sound. Once it has woken me up with its own wild perfume, I start paying attention to other kitchen aromas: What do those sautéing onions smell like—are they still sweet? Does their scent change when I add salt? And when a slightly bitter, acrid note arises (damn!), I know that I've let them burn.

Remembering to open up my senses also opens my imagination and I start exploring new territory. How interesting and full of possibility it is to smell peaches ripening on the table next to a bunch of basil. Can I combine the two for dinner tonight? A salad, maybe, or peach ice cream garnished with candied basil? Or perhaps a peach and basil salsa? Or compote?

I suggest looking for your own equivalent of a bunch of fragrant field basil. Bring it home and plunk it smack in the middle of your kitchen where you can't help but stumble over it. Allow it to remind you to engage all of your senses and to reap the rewards of a body and mind fully present to the perils and magic of life, both in and out of the kitchen.

carrots

don't talk back

even the garlic

submits

yet this isn't about power

really

it's about brightness

and hunger and how day turns into night turns into day again so that

winter gives over to spring so that

the green things can grow—suddenly, fiercely, tenderly—so that

dinner gets made somehow

and the belly is full

and how come I get to be here

and why not potatoes

and what about love and then suddenly and fiercely and tenderly

everything, everywhere, ultimately

always is

RINSHO IKUSHIN

A State of Mind

STEPPING into intimacy through our bodies, through our sense doors, through the basic acknowledgment of our aliveness, is the first step. But we are creatures of the mind as much as (if not more than) creatures of our bodies. In some ways, our bodies are always intimate, for that is their nature: to dwell in the world, to be in contact (with the ground, with objects, with the air, with other people), and to respond.

But what we do with that intimacy internally, how we process it through our thoughts, predilections, personality, and emotions, is often a more complex event. And the kitchen is as much a place of feeling as it is a simple room in our house where cooking occurs. Our relationship to food, to eating, to nourishment, to pleasure and pain, our ideas of scarcity and abundance, of our own worthiness and our sense of responsibility to our families—all of this is present and played out here. The hearth is the heart, and the true nature of the heart cannot be hidden, at least not for long. What's the true nature of your heart? How are you expressing it? What does the world look like to you when you're fully in, responding to its request?

If those questions baffle you, yet at the same time you feel their power as they tug and beckon, then you are hearing their call to intimacy, to a deeper knowing of who you are and how you fit into the world around you. By allowing intimacy to deepen our experience, we create a more informed and therefore a more trustworthy response to our lives. We aren't reacting just to our impulses and neuroses and old, broken patterns. We're relating to the world, face-to-face, in a very direct and meaningful way.

Intimacy can be a difficult request. In order to be intimate, we need to give up control and safety; we need to allow something to be completely what it is and to let it touch us fully, without holding back. Can we do this completely? Can we allow this to happen 100 percent of the time? Some people say that this is the very definition of enlightenment, this unmediated openness to all experience. Maybe so. It's also, as I mentioned on page 39, a definition of madness. But what's more critical, and to me what is more interesting, is not so much chasing after this nearly unattainable goal but simply exploring how intimacy is present (or not) in our own everyday, noisy, messy, busy lives.

So, of course, the kitchen is a good place to do this. Already we are working with keeping our senses awake and open and creating a space that we feel comfortable and safe in. As we engage our bodies with the act of transformation (also known as cooking), we can also practice noticing what comes up when we invite intimacy and seeing what happens when we stay with it.

If you're just starting out on this exploration, it is helpful to emphasize what you are drawn to, what gives you pleasure, what helps you relax and remain available. Once you've stabilized there (and this can be the work of a lifetime), you can begin to explore the less pleasurable things: your aversions, your moments of sadness, your disappointments. Can you be completely present for the frustrated disappointment of a fallen cake or the sad disappointment of being blown off by a lover who never showed for your lovingly cooked dinner? What happens when we touch our more fragile moments with the same care and attention we bring to our pleasures and passions?

How to Begin

As you go about your kitchen, notice what you are drawn to and what you pull away from. Don't judge it or do anything about it. Just notice it. This can be as obvious as pulling your hand away from the hot handle of a pot on the stove or as obscure as the fact that you cringe ever so slightly every time you debone a chicken. It can be as messy and luscious as sucking the last bits of mango off of its pit or as refined as sipping perfectly made green tea from a favorite cup. Whatever it is, see if you can bring a simple, bare attention and awareness to your aversions and attractions.

Above all, try to have this experience of intimacy without doing a single thing with it. Don't move away from it, and don't smother it with your ideas and expectations. Just allow your experience to come forward and then meet it. Let it in, let it be intimate, and don't chase it away with conclusions or opinions. Let it rest, close and intimate. Let it register. And then let this intimacy, this deep knowing and resting in your immediate experience, inform your response to it.

A Small Moment
of Attention and Beauty

THE other day, I was prepping a butternut squash for dinner, an activity that required a fair amount of attention because it involved cutting through something quite hard and slippery with a very sharp knife. This was not a daydreamy kind of activity, like shelling peas or kneading bread dough. I needed to be fully present.

There was the squash strategy to consider, too. To peel or not to peel? (I usually try not to peel.) Peel first and then chop? (Depends on the variety.) How can I get nice, even cubes, especially when negotiating the hollowed-out seed area? (I can't.)

So there I was in my kitchen at the end of an average day, knife in hand and mind focused on the task in front of me. It was a pleasant place to be, at least on that particular afternoon, with oven warmth relaxing my shoulders and the last streaky bits of sunlight scratching at the windowsill.

Soon the whole world was reduced to the rhythmic sound of chopping, the hum/hiss of the gas oven preheating, the last of the fall leaves crackling along the sidewalk below. The orange squash, cut open and sticky, lay next to a turquoise-colored bowl overflowing with a tangle of its strings and seeds. There was a touch of sweat on my brow and my belly rumbled a little, just on the verge of hunger.

It's hard to explain just how perfect this small moment of attention and beauty was. I think the best way to describe it is that there was no desire for things to be different, no wanting for anything, no sense of lack. Just a tiny bit of rumbling in the belly that was soon to be filled and an eyeful of beautiful squash in the tumbling half-light of a day almost over.

These are the moments to pay attention to, these everyday, nothing-special moments where it is possible for a simple but powerful beauty to step forward. Immediate and fleeting, it is not the kind of beauty that can be purchased or engineered or corralled into a picture frame. It can't be created or manipulated, so the trick, if there is one, is to simply pay attention.

The beauty is already there; the only effort needed is to notice it—just a quiet moment of attention and appreciation, and the simple, everyday, and utterly extraordinary song of being alive.

Butternut Squash Roasted in Honey, Chipotle, and Crème Fraîche

Serves 8 as a side dish

Butter for the baking dish and topping

2- to 2½-pound butternut squash

¾ cup crème fraîche or heavy cream

2 teaspoons honey

1 tablespoon canned chipotle in red sauce
(approximately 1 chile, finely chopped)

1 clove garlic, microplaned, pressed,
or very finely minced

½ teaspoon salt

Milk, as needed

1½ cups coarse bread crumbs

Chopped cilantro or parsley for garnish

PREHEAT the oven to 375°F. Butter a 6-cup gratin dish and set aside.

PEEL and seed the butternut squash and cut it into ½-inch cubes. Put the squash cubes into the prepared baking dish, spreading evenly. Cover with foil and bake. After 40 minutes, test the squash to see if it is soft. A knife should easily pierce a piece of squash but it should still have some give. If not, put the foil back on and return to the oven for another 10 minutes or so.

MEANWHILE, in a medium bowl, combine the crème fraîche or cream, honey, chipotle, garlic, and salt. Whisk briskly to combine and set aside. The whisking should help to loosen the texture of the crème fraîche to a thick but pourable consistency. If it doesn't, add a splash of milk.

POUR the cream mixture over the squash, being sure that it is evenly distributed. Sprinkle an even layer of bread crumbs over the top and dot with butter. Bake, uncovered, for another 30 minutes, or until the squash is completely soft and the top is browned.

REMOVE from the oven and let sit for 5 minutes. Garnish with cilantro or parsley and serve.

Note: Also delicious made with sweet potatoes. Peel and slice the potatoes into ¼-inch slices and layer them into the buttered dish, overlapping the slices slightly.

Digging In for the Long Haul: A Few More Words on Meditation

MORNINGS are an excellent time to practice meditation, before our minds have powered up and the challenges of the day have taken over. When we first rise from sleep, we're a little unformed and vulnerable, a little less certain about who we are and where we're going. Our bodies and minds haven't had a chance to fully rev up into the protected state we usually walk around with and call normal. This is an excellent time to sit down and cultivate the ground from which all our thoughts and actions will spring forth for the rest of the day.

The best way to do this is to sit as silently and as still as possible. Just this simple action begins to short-circuit many of our habitual ways of being since virtually all of our waking hours are spent thinking and doing. Meditation is about not thinking and not doing. And that's much, much easier said than done.

But don't let this discourage you! Some people come to meditation with relative ease, but most of us have to work at it (ironic, I know, but true). We have to train our bodies and minds to be able to sit still, to be still. Two things that help with this are consistency and patience. Consistency means sitting down to meditate every day, or nearly every day, even if it's just for 5 minutes. And patience because meditation is not about perfection or achieving goals. It's about digging in for the long haul.

When you first start to meditate, you may be surprised at how many of your thoughts are about the stress of the future or the difficulties of the past. This is your normal, everyday mind just doing its thing. But there is a way to let go of this habit and let your thinking flow, so that it rests lightly here and there, without becoming wrapped up in the tangled nets of pain and gain, of opinions and actions, of past and future.

The most classic way to bring yourself back to the present is to connect with your breathing. Following your breath is helpful because, as long as you are alive, your breath is always with you. Most of us don't have to buy anything or wear anything special in order to breathe. You don't have to have a special certificate or live on a sacred mountaintop. No matter what the circumstances of your life, your breath will always be there. The only thing you need to do is to shift your attention to it. That's it. The easiest/most impossible task ever!

The biggest challenge is to notice when you've forgotten about your breath and started back down the path of your usual, discursive thinking. Just noticing that you're doing this is 90 percent of the effort of meditation. Once you do notice that you've drifted, quietly, gently pull away from those thoughts. Don't yank your mind away, don't berate yourself for drifting or pass judgment on the quality of your meditation. Simply stop the train of thought with an "oh!" or an "oops!" or a "huh." One helpful way to reset your thinking is to notice something neutral in the room around you. I often focus on the light coming through a nearby window.

Another excellent method is to shift the weight of your concentration to listening. A house is seldom completely silent. What do you hear? The refrigerator's hum, maybe? What is coming in from outside? Birdsong, traffic noise, a plane passing overhead? Once you're centered back in the here and now, find your breath. And begin again. And again. And over and over and over again.

Maybe you think meditation isn't for you. Maybe you can't quite bring yourself to sit still and quiet, despite your wish to do so. Or maybe you can do it but find yourself easily drifting from your daily practice. If that's the case, I recommend that you start small, like with the morning tea meditation I shared with you. Of course, this morning meditation is not what you will find in an official meditation center, but it is a start for those of you who have found a period of formal meditation difficult or impossible. So please, if this is the case, try the morning teacup meditation I outline on page 28! In time, you may find that you want even fewer distractions and then can seek out more formal styles of meditation. There are many opportunities to do so these days, either at a meditation center or online.

But don't worry if a less formal, more home-style meditation is what works for you. There is such a thing as being too ambitious with your meditation practice, so don't tangle it up with ideas of gain and betterment. Make just enough effort to sustain your practice and be open to where it takes you, even if it's no further than sitting quietly on your living room floor with a cup of tea in hand.

Kitchen Notebook

THERE'S an old red leather notebook on my kitchen bookshelf, almost invisible in between two rather large and imposing cookbooks. This is my kitchen notebook where I occasionally scrawl out a recipe idea or make notes on something I saw or ate or observed on my travels both around town and farther out. It isn't at all organized or tabulated into sections, there is no rhyme or reason to anything—it's a bit of a brain dump, actually, where I store those random things that I don't want to lose track of but don't have time to neatly organize.

Every now and then, I'll take it down from the shelf and page through it and discover some forgotten inspiration (a chicken liver pâté made with apples and brandy; mint and cilantro chutney; ceviche made with black bass, lime, coconut milk, chile, and mango). Or I'll revisit a jumble of scratches and doodles from planning a long-ago dinner party. Occasionally, there is a list of music or books and films that have caught my eye. An odd quote or poem will show up here and there, or a rough sketch.

Having a kitchen notebook is not a new or unique suggestion. Many people have electronic versions of them these days, with far-flung recipes tagged and filed and pinned along with their guest list and scans of wine labels. But I prefer my analog version, with its wine-spilled crinkled pages and its random order. I like the misspellings and scribbles and wild tangents and higgledy-piggledy disorder. Opening it up is like going on a treasure hunt—what long-forgotten recipe, what unusual suggestion, what memorable dinner party menu will I rediscover this time?

Whenever I open my kitchen notebook, I am so glad that I use one, if only occasionally these days. Life is full, and it's easy to forget the many wonderful, interesting, delicious, inspiring, useful, odd things that come our way. The electronic notebook is very crisp and useful but, for me at least, the hand-scrawled notebook offers an imperfect soulfulness that pushes beyond usefulness into the more messy, circuitous process of creation.

So I encourage the use of a kitchen notebook of some sort, whether you find a more organized electronic approach more helpful or if you're like me and enjoy the messy meanderings of pen and paper.

Chicken Liver Pâté
with Apples and Brandy
Makes about 2 cups

———•

I've been making this pâté since I was very young and working as a baker's apprentice at a French-style bakery in Milwaukee. At first, this pâté was the only way I could eat liver, but as I grew older, it became my gateway into enjoying this very nutritious and delicious food. Equally for special occasions and the casual gathering, this pâté is quite the crowd-pleaser, even among those who claim to hate liver. It can be made ahead of time and frozen, so make up a big batch, and you'll never be without a wonderful treat to offer up.

To serve, simply spread it on thin slices of baguette and garnish with a pretty sliver of apple and a leaf of parsley. Or serve it in a crock with the bread scattered around for quicker presentation. As with most liver pâtés, it's not the prettiest girl at the party, so do try for a nice garnish in order to entice that first bite. After that, your only worry will be if you've made enough.

1½ sticks unsalted butter, at room temperature

1 apple, cored, peeled, and roughly chopped

½ cup chopped shallots

1 pound chicken livers, trimmed

¼ cup brandy (Calvados if you have it)

½ teaspoon dried thyme

Salt and pepper

MELT 2 tablespoons of the butter in a large, wide skillet over medium heat. Add the apple and sauté until it is just starting to brown. Add the shallots and cook for 2 to 3 minutes until they soften, then add the chicken livers, with another tablespoon of butter, if needed. Sauté the livers until they begin to brown on the outsides (but are still somewhat pink within).

ADD the brandy and continue to cook for about 1 minute to heat it up, then turn off the heat. Light a match and, carefully tipping the pan to one side to pool the liquid, cautiously light the brandy. It might give a bit of a whoosh, which may be a little alarming at first, but don't worry, it will quickly die down to a low flame. Flambé the livers, shaking the pan now and then until the flame goes out. Let cool to room temperature. This is important as you don't want the liver mixture to melt the butter when you puree it in the next step.

SPOON the cooled mixture into a food processor fitted with an S blade and process until smooth. Cut the remaining room-temperature butter into chunks and add it to the food processor along with the thyme, a large pinch of salt, and several turns of the peppermill. Process another minute, then taste and adjust the seasonings, as needed. Spoon into containers, cover, and refrigerate for up to a week (or freeze for up to 3 months). This pâté has a lot of butter, so it's best to bring it to room temperature before serving.

Notes: Use an apple that is somewhat tart, such as a Granny Smith or a Jonathan, as the pâté will taste too cloying with a sweeter apple.

Many people run their liver pâté through a sieve after processing as a way to ensure a supersmooth texture. It's a good thing to do if you have a fine sieve rattling about, but if you don't, it will still be fine and fairly smooth if you give it a good run in the food processor.

How to Cook Each and Every Day for the Rest of Your Life

THERE are as many ways to approach the stove as there are ways to kneel and kiss the ground, to paraphrase the poet Rumi. Some of us are optimists, and when we cook, we engage in hope and a desire to nourish, finding pleasure in feeding and being fed, providing ourselves and our loved ones with the strength to carry on, all of which are optimistic notions. Some of us are perhaps a little more pessimistic, although I would argue that cooking well is basically an optimistic endeavor—but is this true? Pessimists, please plead your case!

But sometimes, maybe even often, we cook out of duty. We have a family to feed or some sort of entertaining debt to pay off or even our own bellies to fill. Sometimes the day-in, day-out obligation to get something on the table is nothing more than that: an obligation, especially when purse strings are tight and there's no escaping it through a stop at a restaurant or with takeout. It can feel like drudgery or at least very hard work, and have I used the word "relentless" yet? We only stop eating when we're dead, or nearly dead. So there's really no end to it.

I have no problem with cooking out of duty or drudgery—I hardly expect every single moment of my life to be imbued with the glow of hope and vision and pleasure. And let's face it: Life is largely about maintenance, and eating and cleaning and finding shelter can fall squarely under that category. In fact, it's this "chop wood, carry water" pragmatism that makes cooking all the more enjoyable for me. It grounds me, literally, to the ways in which I am simply an animal on this planet, engaged in something that all animals everywhere are also doing: rustling up something wonderful for dinner.

What to do, then, when your time in the kitchen is boring, when it's just nothing-special, everyday grub? The chopping of another onion, the peeling of carrot after carrot. Another day, another pot roast. In the Zen kitchens I've cooked in, these moments are considered a golden opportunity to wake up to the nature of our conditioned thinking. In Zen, every moment is brand new, and all activity is the ground for awakening. You may be faced with the monumental task of chopping 5-gallon buckets full of vegetables for that afternoon's soup, but each broccoli is a new broccoli, each carrot is very different from the other carrot. So you take the long view and approach the task one carrot, one onion, one broccoli at a time. If you can manage to see that, to stay aware and attentive, there is no boredom, there is no stale routine. Or if there is, it kind of doesn't matter. This is easier said than done, I know (boy, do I know), but it's not impossible.

So awareness, attention, and appreciation can be brought to any task, be it scrubbing the sink or taking out the compost or creating a gorgeous five-layer birthday cake for your best friend. The layer cake may seem more fun and challenging but the truth is, it's all good, it's all life, it's all awakened, precious, alive-on-the-planet activity. You just have to remember to see it that way.

So the next time something you're doing seems like nothing more than obligation and duty, the next time you sigh with boredom at the thought of getting together yet another meal or find yourself wanting to swerve into the Burger King parking lot instead of facing another evening in the kitchen, remember that one of the few things we have control over in this life is our attitude, our perspective, the heft and quality of our mind. Yes, it might be a boring or menial chore but just approach it one chopped onion, one peeled carrot at a time and maybe, just maybe, you'll catch a glimpse of the treasures hidden there.

At the very least, you'll end up with a delicious home-cooked dinner, and what's more precious and necessary than that?

Broad or Deep?

THERE are two basic ways to be proficient in the kitchen: knowing how to cook broadly across many different types of food, methods, and cuisines or mining deeply into being an expert in one area, such as bread-baking or Persian food or desserts. Is one approach better than the other? I would say no. Some people are better at expertise and some at generalization. But it can be fun or useful to push yourself to try something outside of your usual patterns.

Perhaps you're a passionate bread baker. You may spend all of your weekends and many weeknights caring for and feeding your starter and researching hydration percentages. You may know a lot about bread and how to make the best possible loaf, but what about when it comes to serving it? We cannot live on bread alone, so maybe you can take a moment to discover the perfect vinaigrette to dress a lovely salad to serve with your bread. Or perhaps you can master a simple potato leek soup, which can be made with less than five ingredients.

Or what about what goes on top of bread? Can you make your own butter? Maybe one of those robustly flavored olive and garlic tapenades? The deep but narrow tunnel of your expertise is interesting and can offer a lot of satisfaction but try to widen it just a little and see what happens. With just a small effort, you can take your bread-baking from a singular activity into something perhaps a little more nourishing and universal: You can make dinner!

Similarly, a wide and meandering repertoire is useful for variety but is perhaps a bit unfocused. While it's great to have a few pasta and stews and salads under your belt, what would happen if you decided to focus on a single cuisine for a week? Or if you only cooked from one cookbook that has a particular point of view or aesthetic? Going deep into one thing, exploring it thoroughly, is not only fun and interesting, it offers the chance to be focused and disciplined and to discover things you aren't naturally drawn to.

Leaving the comfort of your area of expertise or feeling the restraints of a more focused endeavor can be a challenge, but give it a try, if even just once. Who knows what new truth you may discover about who you are and what you're capable of. These uncharted territories can sometimes be scary and sometimes refreshing, but they will always be instructive.

Potato Leek Soup
with 12 Variations

*This isn't a recipe so much as a walk-through lesson,
kind of a beginning primer for how to cook
using some basic skills and your imagination. I chose
this recipe because it is infinitely simple and
accommodating, with dozens of ways to make it your
own. It's also one of those greater-than-the-sum-
of-its-parts recipes in which a few kitchen staples
and some water come together to create a magical,
even sophisticated, soup. Dive in and enjoy
both the process and the result!*

**Nonwaxy potatoes, such as Russet or
Yukon Gold, scrubbed**

Leeks

Butter

Salt and pepper

YOU'LL want to end up with twice as many potatoes as leeks, more or less. So if you have 2 cups of leeks, have 4 cups of potatoes. Slice the leeks in half vertically and then into thin half-moons horizontally, slicing up through the leek until you reach the rough green section (the smooth pale green section is fine). Put them in a sieve and thoroughly rinse away any dirt and grit. Leave them in the sieve to drain for a minute, then pop them into a saucepan or small Dutch oven with a small hunk of butter.

SAUTÉ the leeks over medium heat, stirring occasionally, until they soften. This usually takes 10 to 15 minutes. Try to avoid browning them, as leeks can easily take on an acrid flavor when overly browned. A little browning here and there is okay.

MEANWHILE, cut up the potatoes. Old-fashioned Russet potatoes are fantastic as well as some of the "gold" varieties. If you want a rough, textured soup, don't peel them; peel them if you want a more refined soup. Cut them into rough cubes and add to the softened leeks.

THEN add enough water to just cover the potatoes plus a large pinch of salt. Bring to a simmer and cook gently until the potatoes start to disintegrate, adding a splash more water, if needed. This can take anywhere from 20 to 40 minutes.

FOR a smooth soup, puree in a blender (carefully! The steam will expand in the jar, so don't fill to the top, and hold the lid on using a tea towel) or do the smart thing:

Acquire and use a stick blender. The easiest route is to simply mash the potato right there in the pot using the back of a wooden spoon until it is a rough puree.

TASTE for salt, which you will likely need, and crack in some fresh pepper. There you have it! Oh, there's a lot you can do from here, but this simple, five-ingredient soup is actually quite delicious just as it is. The truth is if you choose well-grown raw ingredients, scrub them well, and cook them until everything is limp and collapsed, you really can't go wrong. But here is a list, only a beginning really, of where you can go from here.

Add more fat: Swirl in some ghee or olive oil just before serving.

Add dairy: Swirl in sour cream, yogurt, crème fraîche, or cream.

Add acid: Stir some chopped preserved lemon into the dairy before stirring in.

Make it vegan: Use olive or grapeseed oil instead of butter.

Add meat: Garnish with crumbled bacon, crisped pancetta, or sliced sausage.

Add herbs: Garnish with fresh thyme or swirl in a pesto.

Add heat: Drop in a chile de arbol or a pinch of chilli flakes when cooking the leeks.

Add spice: Add a pinch of curry powder or caraway.

Add color: Garnish with a dusting of paprika (smoked, plain, or hot).

Add flavor: Garnish with smoked or truffled salt. Slice a small fennel bulb and cook it along with the leeks.

Switch it up: Substitute sweet potatoes for the regular potatoes.

Make it a miracle: Unexpected guests? You can almost double the quantity of this soup by thinning it with liquid. More water is fine (check again for salt and other flavorings) or even stock, milk, or cream if you're feeling luxurious.

What Kind of Cook Are You?

I once started to take an online quiz but stopped short when it asked me what kind of cook I thought I was. My choices were something like generous (enthusiastic and sharing), methodical (likes long, complex kitchen projects), innovative (goes for the new and unusual), competitive (into impressing and being the best, having the best), or healthy (interested in freshness and nutrition). I was only allowed to pick one, so what I ended up clicking on was the button to take me away from the quiz. Each choice was both too much and not enough, and the idea of choosing just one was frustrating.

Of course, online quizzes aren't the best place to look for your true self, that much has been obvious to me since my preteen years when I would steal my mother's *Cosmopolitan* magazines and secretly take the romantic compatibility tests. But sometimes those quizzes do ask questions that lead one to a deeper consideration. How would I describe myself as a cook? What kind of cook am I?

It didn't take long for me to discover that in no way

was I just one kind of cook. In fact, looking back on that list (generous, methodical, innovative, competitive, healthy), I would've had to click all five choices if I were to be perfectly honest and would probably need several other choices if I really wanted to present a complete picture (lazy, meandering, romantic, practical, curious, and accident-prone come immediately to mind).

But thinking about it even further, the list expands and lengthens because, on some days, I'm a confident expert, knowing exactly what I am doing, and on others, I haven't a clue. Sometimes, I'm the kind of cook who has crackers and cheese for dinner and other times, it's an elaborate soup with fresh-baked bread and a garlicky side salad.

While it's very important to know ourselves, to be aware of our strengths and weaknesses, we also have to be careful not to limit ourselves by our own stories. Declaring yourself to be too impatient of a cook to bake bread or too clumsy of a cook to bone a fish may be (somewhat) true but it's also true that you can be an impatient bread maker and let the bread-making teach you patience, or allow the fish bones to show you grace. In other words, don't let your stories stop you from trying something new, something outside of your usual patterns. Don't let your ideas about who you are dictate who you are.

I leave you with a challenge: Do something against your character today. Try being the kind of cook you're not. Allow yourself to be sloppy if you're neat, or dabble in modernist cuisine if you're usually all about the roast chicken. Think you're a baker and not a cook? Then it's bouillabaisse for you today! Do you never measure anything? Then find a recipe and follow it exactly.

Watch what comes up for you when your stories about what kind of cook you are arise, and watch what happens when you let them go. Notice where there's freedom. Do you find it in the story, or is it in what happens when you let the story go?

Comfort Zones

WE often fall into habits and routines in the kitchen, and it's no wonder: Our lives are busy and it is sometimes easiest to just do what we know best, especially if we have people to feed and not much time to feed them. But these habits, these comfort zones, can also be a trap where we are safe and in control but also perhaps a little bored and uninspired, confined in a routine that is no longer relevant. So it's good to shake things up, if even a little, to bring a fresh and interesting experience to our lives and to our kitchen table and to our bellies.

This doesn't have to be a big shake-up. You can try one new recipe a week or even once a month, and it can be on weekends instead of during the busy workweek. Or pick up one new ingredient each time you do a big grocery shop, and learn everything you can about it, using it as often as possible in your usual dishes. You can also question your assumptions about disliking an ingredient or cuisine, or the notion that you are a cook but not a baker.

Sometimes, switching out your physical space is a

good way to raise some energy. Kitchens are hard places to rearrange, as most of the "furniture" is fixed, but maybe you can add a few shelves or paint the ceiling blue. Or take a weekend like I did recently and rearrange all your cupboards so they make more sense in the flow of how you actually use your kitchen. Something as simple as cleaning out your refrigerator and putting things back in a new configuration can be helpful.

Look for habits. Try to recognize when your behavior or your thinking is just a thoughtless routine and question it: Is it still useful? Does it encourage joyfulness and ease or is it a rut you've fallen into? What happens when you break or disrupt a habit? You might be uncomfortable at first but, given a little time, you may also see new possibilities.

The point is to interrupt a routine that has grown stale and no longer serves you. The point is to remember that this life is not forever, and each moment is a chance to cram in as much experience, as many tastes and textures, as possible. So step into the unknown every now and then, shake things up a little, take a risk with something new. What have you got to lose?

Fearlessness, Failure, and Vulnerability

FEARLESSNESS is an enviable quality, for who doesn't want to stand before the dragon, tall and steady, with sword in hand and bravery in heart? Who doesn't want their lives to be unencumbered by doubt and hesitation, to reap the rare, precious rewards gained from reaching beyond what is known and comfortable and to grasp the prize waiting there?

To be a fearless person means your regrets are few and your accomplishments are vast. You've achieved mastery, knocking all doubts and risks aside as you face the world head-on. When you're fearless, you're the hero and the whole world belongs to you. Right? Wrong.

The first thing to establish is that fearlessness is a myth because even the bravest person is not without fear. In fact, a fearless person is actually a stupid person, for fear can be a wise response to situations where backing off is the more appropriate thing to do.

So fearlessness is less about eradicating our fear and more about how we work with our fear. The kitchen is a perfect place to do this because, let's face it, the things we are afraid of in the kitchen are ultimately more workable than some of the larger fears and challenges life can present. Most of our kitchen fears are little fears, and little fears are a good place to start.

By taking on the simple, non-life-threatening fear of making bread or throwing our first dinner party, we begin to train ourselves in the process of working with fear, of learning how it is possible to experience fear without giving over to it entirely. We learn how fear can be a tool and a teacher and how it is possible for us to stand reasonably strong and upright even while it is trying its hardest to render us small and immobile.

So where to begin? What's the best tool, the important bit of kitchen magic needed to overcome your culinary anxieties? Become a fan, a follower—a fervent disciple!—of failure, for fear of failure is often at the root of all our kitchen fears.

———•—•—•———

For all my trilling on and on about the pleasures and passions of life in the kitchen, I am also quite aware that the kitchen can be an unforgiving place, where we risk a whole array of mistake-making events every time we enter. Even from the most simple activity of picking up a knife and assembling a few ingredients for a salad there are just so many ways things can go wrong. Too much or not enough garlic in the dressing, too much or not enough salt or pepper. Gritty lettuce, soapy-tasting carrots, over-roasted nuts. Soggy/dry, too tart/too sweet, overdone/raw, boring/overworked—there are so many mistakes to make! So many failures to encounter and endure! Find yourself in the kitchen and you will discover what your relationship to failure is because there are a million ways to fail there.

The revelation is that this is good news, really good news, in fact. Because if you accept from the beginning that you will fail, you will have given yourself a gift: the freedom to fail. This freedom will enable you to be bold and curious and relentless in your pursuit of deliciousness, characteristics that will likely lead to some very delightful results. Those delightful results will in turn boost your confidence, and that extra confidence will help diminish some of the fear.

So set yourself up for failure and have at it! Any cook who tells you that she never makes mistakes or acts so arrogant that she seems invincible is not your friend in the kitchen. All the best cooks fail—often, spectacularly, and without apology.

———————•———

Still, it must be recognized that failure is difficult for us. There are a lot of reasons for this but one of them is that failure makes us feel vulnerable, exposed, foolish. This vulnerability can tenderize us if we let it, or it can do the opposite and make us tough and withdrawn. It's your choice and an important one, for in a very real and visceral way, how vulnerable you are will dictate how you will live and experience your life. Are you available and tender or cold and shut down? Aware, upright, and clear-eyed or guarded and suspicious?

Vulnerability is difficult for us because we feel exposed, and to be exposed is to be susceptible to danger. But we have to get over that. I remember when I was going through a tough time and was quite withdrawn, protected, and not very happy. A friend would invite me out on walks with her little puppy, and as we wandered the streets of San Francisco, we would encounter all sorts of other dogs, most of them much, much bigger than our pup. Every time this would happen, Biscuit (the puppy) would wag her tail and roll onto the ground and expose her belly. Every time. It didn't matter if the other dog was a mighty pit bull or a bouncing terrier, she would wiggle and squirm in excitement and roll over on her back and show off her belly. The other dogs would respond by wagging their tails right back and licking her face in excitement, and in less time than it takes to say "down, boy!", she would have made herself a new best friend.

One day, as my friend and I were watching this happen for what felt like the hundredth time, she looked over at me and said, "That's what you need to do. You need to remember how to roll on your back and show your belly and let the big, bad, scary thing lick your face." While I found that image simultaneously difficult and hilarious, I got her point. It was time to take some risks, to crack the shell, and let some light in. It was time to start showing my belly.

So we're vulnerable when we make mistakes, and we're vulnerable, too, when we allow intimacy into our lives. When we practice this, when we begin to bring attention and appreciation to our everyday encounters, when we drop some of our defensive posturing and allow the bright simple truths of the moment to step forward, we also encounter who we are in ways that maybe we've never touched before. There's a different, brighter light shining on us, and it is exposing those dark corners, bringing forth what we've kept hidden. This can be a little startling, maybe even a little unnerving.

Once again, the kitchen is a good place to play around with this less familiar way of being. Kitchens are usually warm and friendly places where the worst that can happen is that you screw up a meal and will have to order in a pizza. (Unless you manage to burn down the house—that might be the worst thing, but let's agree it's not likely to happen.) Kitchens are a safe place for us to open up and make some beautiful messes and interesting mistakes.

So get into the kitchen and practice with making mistakes, practice with being vulnerable. Bring in some of that bright light of awareness and let it shine in the dark corners. Allow yourself to be made just a little more whole by what you find there.

The Perfect Salad
(or How to Dress a Salad without Measuring Anything)

●

Many years ago, I read a recipe on how to dress a simple green salad in Crescent Dragonwagon's The Dairy Hollow House Cookbook. *And when I say read, I mean read—this was no prim list of ingredients and instructions, this was a multipage, very specific, and very detailed manifesto. Intrigued, I followed her instructions and indeed, the resulting salad was spectacular. To this day, this is how I make a green salad 95 percent of the time. It has never failed, and it always receives the highest compliments.*

Here is my version of Crescent Dragonwagon's The Salad.

Lettuce

Olive oil

Garlic

Vinegar or a whole lemon

Salt

Pepper (optional)

THE LETTUCE

CHOOSE your lettuce carefully—it must be fresh and full of flavor. Of course, you can make this salad with those time-saving plastic bags of prewashed greens, and it will be just fine. But it won't be spectacular. The types of lettuces and greens are entirely up to you, based on what you like, what you are serving, and what's available. How much lettuce depends on how many people you are serving, if this is going to be a side or a main dish, and if you are adding additional ingredients. In general, one or two large handfuls per person are a good place to start.

THE most important thing is that the lettuce is well washed, grit-free, and very, very dry. This cannot be emphasized enough. I usually fill up a dishpan full of cold water, add the lettuce, give it a swish, and let it sit for a minute or two so that the grit settles to the bottom. If the lettuce is very dirty, I may repeat this step. Then I carefully lift it out of the water and into a salad spinner.

AFTER spinning, the lettuce is spread out on tea towels, which are then rolled up in order to blot up every last stray drop of moisture. The tea towel rolls are an excellent way to store the lettuce in the refrigerator, as the lettuce-washing step is one of those things you can do a day in advance (but no more than a day!).

THE OLIVE OIL AND GARLIC

USE the best olive oil your budget allows and the freshest garlic you can buy. Olive oils generally fall into two categories: the good stuff for cooking and using in recipes where other flavors will dominate, and the extrawonderful stuff for using in salads and as a finishing oil. Use the extra-wonderful stuff here, if you can. You won't need much.

CHOOSE a smallish clove of garlic. This is not about overwhelming the salad with garlic intensity, it's about a balance of flavors. There is a world of difference between fresh, creamy, sweet, plump, moist garlic cloves (the ideal) and old, dried, browning, acrid garlic cloves. Make sure the garlic is as close to ideal as possible. Some people remove the tiny green sprout that can sometimes be found pushing up through the middle of the clove and some people don't. I remove it.

POUR a small amount of olive oil into a large bowl. (This can be the bowl you are planning on serving the salad in.) I usually start with a small glug or two. Don't worry—you can add more later. Add finely chopped garlic, or press or rasp the clove directly into the oil. Stir it up with your finger so that the garlic is coated with oil and leave it to marinate for 10 minutes or so. This is a good time to prep any extras you are adding to your salad.

THE TOSS

HAVE the lettuces and any additions handy. If you are using lemon, cut it in half. If you are using vinegar, have the bottle handy with the cap off. Add a good pinch of salt to the oil. It won't dissolve but the oil helps to evenly distribute the salt. I like to use a flakey sea salt such as Maldon for its crunchy texture.

ADD your perfectly dried lettuce leaves to the bowl and toss gently using only one hand. This is important! You want your other hand clean and dry so you can add more ingredients. If the salad needs more oil, this is the time to add it (using that dry, clean hand). All the lettuce leaves should be coated in the thinnest film of oil, so be sure to toss gently but thoroughly.

THE ACID

NOW is the time to add the acid—usually vinegar or lemon juice. Sprinkle a small amount of vinegar over the lettuce leaves, starting with 1 to 2 teaspoons. If you are using a lemon, squeeze some over the leaves, starting with half a lemon. Give the lettuce a few tosses to distribute the vinegar or lemon.

THE TASTE

TASTE a leaf. What does it need? More salt? This will bring the flavors forward and give them a boost. More acid? This will brighten and enliven the flavors. Does it need more oil? This will smooth out and balance any excess sharpness from the vinegar or lemon.

ALMOST DONE

ONCE you have the balance of salt, acid, and fat right, you are basically done. You can serve this salad right now, just as it is. And, of course, you can add all sorts of things, too. For instance, I usually add freshly ground pepper at this point (ground into a little bowl just before I made the salad so I can still use my tossing hand or ground right there on the spot by any lucky person who just happens to be passing through the kitchen).

THE EXTRAS

OF course, there are all sorts of extras you can add at this point. Depending on what they are, they will affect the acid/salt/fat balance a little so be sure to taste after you add them and adjust by adding in a little more of what's needed for balance. Adding avocado, for instance, will up the fat/creamy factor, so a little more salt and a drop of lemon might be good.

TO SERVE

AS mentioned, you can make this salad in the bowl you are serving it in, which has a nice practical sense of economy. I used to do this all the time until I discovered that a platter or a wide, shallow bowl is actually better for serving salad as it prevents "sinkers"—those heavy extra ingredients that tend to sink to the bottom of a deep bowl.

FOR a dinner party, where you want to have as little last-minute work as possible, try this handy trick: Add the olive oil/garlic/salt to the bowl and then gently lay the salad greens on top. Cut open the lemon and leave it next to the bowl. When it comes time to serve the salad, simply toss the greens in the oil, then sprinkle on the lemon and pepper, and toss again. Voilà! You will have a delicious dressed salad in less than 30 seconds.

AND that is another reason to try this salad method— no extra dressing pooling at the bottom of the bowl; no soggy, overly dressed greens—just a perfectly balanced, perfectly dressed salad made with minimal fuss. The perfect salad.

Notes: If you usually like mustard in your vinaigrette, then add a small plop to the olive oil in the beginning.

The garlic is optional (I guess) but try to use it if possible.

If you want to use minced shallots, add them to the oil along with the garlic in the beginning.

However, if your garlic or shallots are very strong, toss them with the vinegar instead of the oil. Make this your first step so they have some time to sit in the vinegar, which will mellow them.

Cooking with Heart

IN cooking, like in many things in life, there's technique and then there's heart. One is driven by dedication and discipline and the other by the desire to connect and express love. Is one more important than the other? Are they opposites? Two sides of the same coin? Mutually supportive? What's more important to you: the perfect bowl of soup or the person you're serving it to?

When I think about technique, I think about mastery and skill and precision. I think of years of disciplined study and dedication, hours and hours of practice and refinement. Mastering technique requires patience and the ability to focus on the long view. I have a great deal of admiration and respect for someone who can deliver their talents in such a carefully crafted vehicle. Like watching those TV talent shows, it's thrilling to see someone at their pinnacle, their talent honed and polished until it is as precise and perfect as possible.

Heart, on the other hand, is about love, a wilder, more unrestrained expression. It comes when you relax and allow your actions to come from somewhere deep inside, guided by the basic human need for connection and expression. Heart is often messy, for it isn't overly concerned with discipline, and it is often impatient for it "knows what it wants." It can be very tender, too. If technique is a TV contestant, then heart is a young musician alone on the stage for the first time, his eyes squeezed shut and his voice wavering with emotion.

Of course, technique and heart don't have to live on opposite sides of the room. In fact, in ideal conditions, they actually support each other. Technique and precision can give heart a steady platform in which to shine bright and heart can remove some of the eye-blinding glare off of technique and allow for connection. Ideally, they will be both be present, and when that happens, it's golden.

The kitchen, like the stage, is a natural place for technique and heart to find their balance. If a cook is all about technique, if he concerns himself solely with competence and the tyranny of precision, then he is blind to the basic reason for cooking. He will have missed the very precious opportunity to engage in one of life's most pleasurable acts: to cook with love, for love. And his food will reflect this. It will look gorgeous and probably taste really good, but something essential will be missing.

But it's also true that knowing the best way to handle your ingredients and utensils, knowing how and when to add salt or how finely to chop the onion, is necessary to make something that is truly delicious. If you want to connect and express your heart, wild and willful as it is, then you need a container, something to hold it steady so that your expression can be met and appreciated.

If you love someone, then you want them to be happy. And good food, prepared with attention and care, will always be a way to make someone smile, be it a complex, multilayered dinner party dish or a bowl of perfectly cooked oatmeal eaten in bed on a foggy morning, with just the right amount of salt and maple syrup and, of course, served and eaten with love.

How to Be Angry
in the Kitchen

I'M not often angry but when I am, I can feel the energy bouncing around inside of me like a wild beast, and the only thing I can focus on is the urgent need to let that tiger out. Slamming things like doors and dinner plates is one way to do it, although that can create a whole new set of problems. Yelling, too, offers a release but it can also cause a lot of grief: When the tiger speaks for me, I usually regret it for a long, long time.

Anger is an emotion of rejection. It has a hard time sharing the room with intimacy although it can be said that we only get angry when we really care, when something or someone matters enough to us. But still, when we're angry, something is happening that we do not like, and in a very forceful way, we want it to go away.

People often deal with their anger in two ways: either flying off the handle or trying to smooth it over. Either way, we just don't want to feel what we're feeling anymore. But when life's circumstances conspire in a way that is deeply unjust, sometimes anger can be the appropriate response. So our anger can actually be worthy of exploration, if only we can find a way to be clear-eyed in the middle of its messiness and reactivity.

Anger contains within it its own antidote, a clue to resolution and peace. Somewhere in the middle of all that heat and mayhem, there's a truth that's perhaps a little too much to take but still necessary to know. We need to see clearly into anger even when we're caught up in it. Tricky stuff. It's hard to find this clarity when you're throwing a head of cabbage across the room. The release is there, but the opportunity for insight is lost.

It may be difficult to imagine, but this is a good time to go into the kitchen and find something to do that's useful and physically engaging, something that allows for vigorous and exhausting movement, like kneading bread. This way, anger's energy is diverted to something productive, and the mind has an opportunity to engage the root cause of the situation in a less reactive way. Or maybe your habit is to stuff the anger before it can bloom and get you into trouble? The solution is actually the same. By taking on a vigorous task, we can coax the anger out into the light of day, giving us an opportunity to reflect before immediately channeling it back into the activity.

So when you find yourself in the realm of anger, don't lean into it and don't back away from it. It's only by standing straight up in the middle of the fire that you will find the nugget of truth that truly releases you. The trick is to stay connected to your anger without being controlled by it, and one way to do that is to go into the kitchen, roll up your sleeves, and start beating the hell out of something delicious.

Suggestions for Beating the Hell Out of Something Delicious

Whip cream using only a hand whisk, a
clean bowl, and all the strength available
in your dominant arm.

Skip the electric mixer and cream the
butter and sugar in a sweet recipe
with a wooden spoon.

Finely shred and then squeeze
and knead and pummel a head of
cabbage for sauerkraut.

Try your hand at *gougères*, a French cheese
puff that requires beating several eggs into
a sticky dough until it is smooth.

Make Southern-style beaten biscuits,
which require 20 minutes of being
whacked with a hammer (30 minutes
if they're for company).

Make mayonnaise by hand.

Make bread or fresh pasta;
both require kneading.

Get out the mortar and pestle and
crush or grind away.

A Small Jar of Sauerkraut

Many people don't know that making sauerkraut
requires a great deal of physical energy, making
it a perfect anger-management tool. After the
cabbage has been shredded and salted, one must
knead it and squeeze it hard until it completely
surrenders and becomes a limp, wet, broken mass.
There's something very satisfying in picking up a
large heap of cabbage and twisting and squishing
it between your hands. This is especially useful for
when you're feeling overly imaginative and your
anger is directed at a particular person.

1 smallish head cabbage (about 3 pounds)

1 generous tablespoon sea salt (not iodized salt)

REMOVE any wilted or discolored outer leaves from the cabbage. Cut it into quarters and cut out the core. Slice the cabbage into ribbons, about medium thickness like for coleslaw.

IN a large bowl, combine the cabbage and the salt. You'll want a fairly large bowl, so you can really get your hands in there and work. Using clean hands, start to knead the cabbage, pressing and squeezing it between both hands. Be vigorous! The cabbage will soon wilt and soften and begin to extrude liquid. After a while, you will notice that you have quite a bit of liquid and that the cabbage is completely limp.

USING your hands, scoop the cabbage up and press it into a sterilized 2-quart widemouthed canning jar. If you can fit your fist into the jar, press the cabbage down as you go. If your hand doesn't fit into the jar, use a wooden spoon or the pestle from your mortar and pestle to really pack the cabbage into the jar. You will notice that this raises the liquid above the cabbage mass, which is a good thing. In order to prevent spoilage, the cabbage needs to remain completely submerged in the brine. The jar will not be full to the top, which is fine.

POUR any juices from the bowl into the jar and tamp it down one more time. There may be a few floating pieces of cabbage—try to push them into the brine. Some people will fold up a large cabbage leaf and shove it in to keep the cabbage shreds down. I find that they generally stay submerged without too much fuss. Another hint is to not shred your cabbage into teeny-tiny pieces as these are the bits that tend to want to float.

COVER the jar with a cloth napkin or other densely woven fabric and pop on a rubber band to secure. Leave on your kitchen counter for several days, checking at least once a day to push down any floating cabbage shreds. The longer the cabbage sits, the stronger it will get. Start tasting it at day seven. If you like it, then replace the cloth cover with a lid and refrigerate. (Discard the whole cabbage leaf, if using.) Most sauerkraut will start to become flavorful by 1 week but many people let it sit longer to further develop flavor and beneficial bacteria, up to 1 month or longer. Refrigeration will stop this process, so let it go as long as possible before refrigerating it.

SOMETIMES, a thin layer of white "bloom" will appear on the top of the brine. No worries, just do your best to spoon this off. It is very rare for sauerkraut to go off, but if it does, it will be quite obvious: It will smell horrible (not the usual funky kraut smell), sometimes even turning colors and becoming slimy or mushy. If this happens, throw it away and start over.

Note: This is a simple, entry-level approach to making your own sauerkraut. Once you have this mastered, or if you find you really enjoy fermenting and want to explore other vegetable ferments, you may want to invest in special equipment like a fermentation crock or an airlock. (These can easily be purchased online.) You can also explore adding other vegetables and flavorings such as caraway, dill, lemon, shredded carrots or beets, or fennel.

Being Agile

THE kitchen can challenge us in ways beyond a pulled lower back or the ability to create a complex lattice crust for a pie. Cooks need to be quick thinkers in order to respond to sudden or expected changes or to problem-solve all manner of ingredient malfunctions: underripe tomatoes, flavorless chicken, spoiled cream. Clocking in lots of time at the stove is the best solution for these challenges, for if we cook enough, we develop the skill and sensibility to handle almost anything that comes our way. And if that isn't the case, a quick Internet search can fill in the blanks.

But there is also an inner agility, a certain nimbleness in our emotional response to kitchen challenges that is helpful beyond the basic mechanics of cooking. The synonyms for the word *agile* have an appealing, playful quality: Who doesn't want to be fleet-footed, nimble, or lithe? Reaching high, bending low, and dodging the family dog can make a ballet out of some meal prep (at least in my imagination!), but even so, physical agility is less important than the inner agility of the mind and heart. After all, some of us are less graceful and limber than others but still can manage a decent four-course meal if given half a chance. But none of us could pull that off (and still retain our sanity) if we didn't have an inner flexibility, the ability to be resourceful and quick-thinking as we juggle the dozens of priorities and decisions needed just to get dinner on the table.

How do you bring this inner agility to your kitchen, and into your whole life for that matter? It begins with an overarching sense of generosity and availability. When difficulty arises, instead of contracting around the problem and burrowing deeper into confusion and upset, we open to it as possibility. What can I do now? What's available? What's possible? We generously allow the problem to become a moment of creativity, and in the spaciousness of this, we find a solution. Maybe we can pivot gracefully toward it, or maybe it's more of a fumble and a save situation, but it doesn't stop us from figuring it out, moving forward, and getting things done.

Practice

TO practice something means to perform an activity over and over again until we become proficient at it. At least that's one definition, but I would say that it's only half of it. For me, practice is doing something over and over so that we reach proficiency, and then we keep going, keep practicing to go beyond proficiency into a more intimate state where the activity becomes who we are—and who we are is that activity. And then we keep practicing to deepen this, and because we can never be done with deepening, we keep practicing. And since who we are has become intimate with this activity, we are never not practicing.

In other words, we begin by learning the mechanics until, over time, we merge with the activity but we never stop learning, deepening, and becoming. This is just as true for playing the violin as it is for making soup or anything we do, including the whole symphony of simple activities it takes to live a life. When we notice, appreciate, and deepen our experiences, everything we do becomes practice. This is what it means to live a whole-hearted life.

When we approach our lives as practice, we can relax a little, for we aren't so caught up in a final judgment, in striving toward an end point. We're not so concerned with mastery. We see our lives as a process, which gives us much more room to experiment, to fail and recover, to meander and discover. Besides, as anyone who has been called a master knows, practice never stops no matter how proficient you become.

So kitchen practice simply means bringing care and attention to everything we do. Some things are more exciting, some things are more mundane, but we still tend to them all with equal regard. It means showing up for whatever arrives and meeting it with clarity and a gentle heart. It means we cultivate the capacity to notice and appreciate the circumstances of our lives, and to be steady and sturdy in the midst of difficulty.

It's important to not be too precious here: In the end, it's just dinner, after all. It's the humbleness of this that's inspiring, not the specialness. An old Zen master once said that if you pick up a leaf of chard in this way, it will be like picking up a 16-foot golden Buddha. Likewise, a 16-foot golden Buddha is no more precious than a simple leaf of chard. The ordinary and the extraordinary manifesting in one gesture, in one activity, in one, simple, everyday, human life.

A Quick, Busy-Week
Dinner for One (or Many)

—●—

These days, there are very few people who don't
understand the difficulty of coming home from work,
tired and depleted, only to be confronted with the
exhausting task of getting dinner on the table. This is
just as true for the solo cook as for those of us who
have a family to feed. The occasional frozen pizza is
nothing to be ashamed of, but most of us don't want
pizza as our steady diet. So we need a short list of
go-to meals that are quick and easy and delicious and
healthy, too. This dish, which consists of heating up
some greens and veg with a handful of cooked beans
and topping it with an egg, is a favorite as it is
very quick and easy and delicious, too.

I wrote a lot of this book while sitting in cafés, of
which I am blessed to have many in my Oakland,
California, neighborhood. This dish is based on one that
is always on the menu at the Boot and Shoe Service café
that has often sustained and inspired me. It is simple,
hearty, and comforting. At Boot and Shoe, they have
a wood-fired oven to cook the dish in, which is won-
derful but certainly not possible in my home kitchen.
Luckily, this stovetop method works just as well.

Guilt in the Kitchen

THE kitchen, for me, is usually a place of joy and refuge where I can be creative, experimental, expressive, and accomplished. Even better, it's also an ordinary place where the most basic of human activities—cooking and eating—are enacted every day. I love the ordinary/extraordinary synergy of cooking and am often quite pleased that we need to indulge in this necessity on a fairly frequent basis. (Read: Everyday!)

So when something like guilt arises in the kitchen, I've learned to pay attention. Why is this icky feeling messing with my bliss? And what am I going to do about it?

Our kitchens can be one of the most guilt-inducing places in our homes. We feel guilty about what we're eating (too many carbs, too much sugar, not enough veg). Or we feel guilty about buying all those leafy vegetables and then tossing them in the trash when they've gone bad, which leads to guilt about not having a compost bin, which leads to even more guilt about not single-handedly saving our planet.

Guilt in the Kitchen

THE kitchen, for me, is usually a place of joy and refuge where I can be creative, experimental, expressive, and accomplished. Even better, it's also an ordinary place where the most basic of human activities—cooking and eating—are enacted every day. I love the ordinary/extraordinary synergy of cooking and am often quite pleased that we need to indulge in this necessity on a fairly frequent basis. (Read: Everyday!)

So when something like guilt arises in the kitchen, I've learned to pay attention. Why is this icky feeling messing with my bliss? And what am I going to do about it?

Our kitchens can be one of the most guilt-inducing places in our homes. We feel guilty about what we're eating (too many carbs, too much sugar, not enough veg). Or we feel guilty about buying all those leafy vegetables and then tossing them in the trash when they've gone bad, which leads to guilt about not having a compost bin, which leads to even more guilt about not single-handedly saving our planet.

There's guilt for not producing enough delicious, healthy meals for our families; guilt for not buying organic, free-range, local; guilt for not doing the dishes or mopping the floor or defrosting the freezer. Guilt—what a nuisance!

But first, I want to point out that guilt is not always such a bad thing. Our guilty feelings are simply telling us that our ideas and expectations are not aligned with what's actually happening. This can be helpful information. It can be an indicator to pause, take stock, and adjust accordingly. If we can do this simply and straightforwardly, our situation easily becomes more manageable. Guilt has a helpful, if limited, place in our kitchens and lives.

But guilt rarely travels alone. It's often accompanied by a sense of shame, inadequacy, and frustration. So while it's okay to feel the initial pinprick of guilt's lesson, it's not okay to indulge it or, just as bad, to ignore it. Unchecked, guilt goes underground and can undermine the simple pleasures and satisfactions inherent in being alive. When you feel guilt rising, try to check it before a whole story blooms up around it and anchors itself to you. Ask yourself what the expectations are and what is keeping you from meeting them. Don't indulge the notion that it is some shortcoming on your part. Often it's just a simple matter of logistics and adjusted expectations. Ask yourself, "What is doable? What is workable given the circumstances of my life?" and take it from there.

Guilt is quite a tenacious and sometimes even habitual response for some of us, and it's not always possible to simply shrug it off. And of course, the last thing we need to feel is guilty about feeling guilty! So small steps, baby steps are helpful. See if you can take one or two spoonfuls of that amazing cream soup, or a few chews of that crispy bacon, and just enjoy it in that moment. Often, by registering that pleasure deeply, we find that we are satisfied and don't need more. If veg-centric, healthy meals are your goal, begin with the understanding that they take more time and effort and explore to what degree you can manage them—maybe just once or twice a week, or maybe you'll find that an hour or so of prep work on a Sunday evening makes all the difference.

We can never eradicate guilt from our lives completely but we can keep it in its place. We can limit its negative effects on our lives, while at the same time using its keen ability to judge and measure to our advantage. The kitchen, with its endless opportunities to promote guilt and dissatisfaction, is an excellent place to explore and practice this.

A Quick, Busy-Week
Dinner for One (or Many)

These days, there are very few people who don't understand the difficulty of coming home from work, tired and depleted, only to be confronted with the exhausting task of getting dinner on the table. This is just as true for the solo cook as for those of us who have a family to feed. The occasional frozen pizza is nothing to be ashamed of, but most of us don't want pizza as our steady diet. So we need a short list of go-to meals that are quick and easy and delicious and healthy, too. This dish, which consists of heating up some greens and veg with a handful of cooked beans and topping it with an egg, is a favorite as it is very quick and easy and delicious, too.

I wrote a lot of this book while sitting in cafés, of which I am blessed to have many in my Oakland, California, neighborhood. This dish is based on one that is always on the menu at the Boot and Shoe Service café and has often sustained and inspired me. It is simple, hearty, and comforting. At Boot and Shoe, they have a wood-fired oven to cook the dish in, which is wonderful but certainly not possible in my home kitchen. Luckily, this stovetop method works just as well.

All in all, this dish takes maybe 10 minutes to prepare. It makes a perfect busy week dish because you don't have to chop anything—there's no onion or garlic or any mincing to do. It is infinitely flexible in your choice of beans, greens, and veg. It is also very flexible in regard to flavors. Feel free to add a pinch of your favorite spice (cumin is a popular one in my household), or start the whole process by sautéing a sliced sausage in the pan, then adding the greens. A few tablespoons of chopped parsley or basil to finish is also good, but not necessary. If you didn't add any chili oil or are adverse to spicy things, a few drops of balsamic vinegar or lemon juice will brighten things.

To make this for two, just double the ingredients. In fact, with a large skillet, you could probably increase it to four or six and feed the whole gang.

Greens

Olive oil

Salt

1 cup cooked chickpeas or other beans

Chili oil

1 egg

IN a small skillet, wilt a few handfuls of greens in a splash of olive oil. The greens can be kale or spinach or whatever you have around. Just toss them in the oil, keeping the heat at medium, until they shrink and collapse. Sprinkle on a nice big pinch of salt while you're at it.

ADD the beans. They can be beans from a can or beans you've cooked yourself. Let's be honest: The beans you cooked yourself will be better in taste and texture, but the beans that come from a can are a more likely choice if your week's been busy. Either one is fine. Just be sure to drain the canned variety. Chickpeas are my usual choice for the dish but almost any bean will do: black beans, pinto beans, white beans.

COOK, shaking the pan and stirring gently so as not to break up the beans, until they are heated through. Add a little olive oil if the pan is too dry. You can also add any cooked leftover vegetables at this point. Roasted carrots or parsnips or cauliflower are good or cubes of roasted squash. Roasted asparagus in the spring is a really tasty treat. Sprinkle on some hot chili oil, to taste.

MAKE a little shallow well in the middle of the mixture and crack an egg into it. Cover the pan, lower the heat a little, and continue to cook until the egg white is set but the yolk is still runny—or however you like your egg done, although the runny yolk creates a very nice sauce for this dish. Remove the lid and drizzle with a final touch of olive oil and a pinch of crunchy salt.

TO serve, carefully wiggle a spatula under the bean mixture where the egg is and scoop everything up and onto a plate. Be sure the egg is centered on the spatula as this helps to avoid breaking the yolk. Then scoop up the rest of the beans and scatter them around the egg. (Or you can just leave everything in the skillet and eat it straight from there.) Serve with some crusty bread on the side to sop up any juices.

On Letting It Go

WE all know and understand that we're not supposed to cry over spilled milk, and yet sometimes we do because sometimes spilled milk sucks, or it's the last straw in a series of challenges and difficulties that day. Or because we really wanted that milk and now it's gone. It's easy to say "Don't cry, just take a breath and let it go," but it's often much harder to actually do it, especially when we're so caught up in the situation that it's too late for deep breaths and mindful pauses.

Our time in the kitchen is rife with opportunities to practice letting go. There's the obvious spilled milk (and the ten thousand other spilled, dropped, knocked over, and shattered things). There's also the milk that boils over and burns a thick, stinky layer of scorched goo onto the clean stovetop. There's the milk that's curdled, or the milk that's low-fat when the recipe calls for whole, or the tres leches cake that was a complete failure. There's the milk that someone forgot to buy, or drank up without asking, or left out on the counter to sour.

Sometimes, it's because of a disaster, sometimes a mere disappointment or inconvenience but still, it's not unusual to find ourselves in the middle of a meltdown in the kitchen. What do we do with our feelings when we're caught in the middle of feeling them? How can we just let it go when there's a ball of anger or frustration or sadness caught in our throats? Do we swallow it or spit it out in a spew of curse words? What is the most helpful thing to do when we're in the midst of reactivity?

This is why the kitchen is such a great place to practice letting go. Notice I said *practice* letting go, which doesn't always mean *actually* letting go. We may try to let it go and yet we may find ourselves unable to do so, not one bit. Or we may want to let it go but discover that some stuff can be dropped, but not all of it.

The practice of letting go means bringing as much awareness and kindness that we can to the situation and then responding. It means letting go of as much as we can—mourning the loss, but letting go of the anger, for instance. Sometimes, it will be appropriate to quietly let it go. This may or may not be easy, but you will know it is appropriate because it will feel right.

But sometimes, with as much of that awareness and kindness as we can muster, we will have to address the situation. We may have to speak to our spouse or child or friend. We may have to speak to ourselves, or even to that bottle of curdled milk. We may be talking out loud or muttering to ourselves or be silent, but we will not be letting it go. Because letting it go, at least in this stage of the game, is not the best response.

One of the deepest wisdoms we can cultivate is the wisdom of responding appropriately to the joys and pains that make up our daily lives. There is no formula for doing this, there is no "if A, then B" because life is just too unpredictable and ever-changing. Some days we swallow and some days we spew and some days we manage to find that narrow but precious place that allows us to both contain and express our feelings.

So why is the kitchen such a great place for practicing letting go? Well, as just mentioned, it's always going to give us ample opportunities to do so, no matter how careful we are. And besides, while they may be disappointing or frustrating, most of our kitchen disasters are usually small and workable. Spilled milk is, after all, just spilled milk.

But, for me, it's also because the kitchen is a place of alchemy and magic. Surrounded by the continuous surrendering of the raw into the cooked, the whole into the torn, the bland into the succulent, I cannot help but be inspired by the examples shown there. They teach me, over and over, how letting go enables transformation and how transformation—this plain, everyday kitchen magic—is what sustains my life.

So be it spilled milk or a ruined dinner or a difficult encounter with a loved one, I hope I'm able to respond with as much wisdom and kindness as possible. I hope I can transform a difficulty into something more spacious, something that allows for the hard and noble work of letting go and getting out of the way and allowing the next moment to arrive, free and unencumbered and completely brand new.

Dinner Can Be Many Things

WE'VE talked about how not everything we cook can be fabulous and how feeling guilty in the kitchen is not a good way to go. So what are some simple things to make on those nights when you're late or tired or completely uninspired (or all three)?

First, remember that dinner does not have to be elaborate. Scrambled eggs and toast make a quick, delicious meal. If you feel the need to add some vegetables, then wilting down a few handfuls of kale in olive oil isn't too much extra effort. Finish with a splash of lemon juice or chili oil to brighten things up and voilà! You're done.

Soup for dinner is just fine, especially if you have homemade in your freezer. A superquick, simple soup from scratch can be made with hot water and miso paste. Yes, miso soup is usually made with *dashi* (a Japanese stock) instead of plain water, but plain water will do in a pinch. Stir in small cubes of tofu or leftover vegetables, also cubed. (The chopping can be done in the time it takes to heat the water.) Or shred some cooked chicken and add a few leaves of baby spinach, which will cook quickly in the hot broth. These are far from traditional additions, of course, but what matters most here is getting dinner on the table.

Assembling is another good way to go. Gather many different things from your fridge and pantry: hard-boiled eggs, a wedge of cheese, a few pickled things, a miscellany of sausage ends and leftover meats. Olives. A pot of mustard. Some roasted nuts. A sliced apple or pear. Add a loaf of good crusty bread (or flatbread or crackers), and you have a meal.

The point is that dinner can be many things, depending on what's available in terms of time and ingredients and energy. Dinner doesn't always have to be something you're going to want to take a photo of, and it doesn't always have to be interesting or exciting or new. Just do your best within the present circumstances and enjoy.

Red Brocade

NAOMI SHIHAB NYE

The Arabs used to say,
When a stranger appears at your door,
feed him for three days
before asking who he is,
where he's come from,
where he's headed.
That way, he'll have strength
enough to answer.
Or, by then you'll be
such good friends
you don't care.
Let's go back to that.
Rice? Pine nuts?
Here, take the red brocade pillow.
My child will serve water
to your horse.
No, I was not busy when you came!
I was not preparing to be busy.
That's the armor everyone put on
to pretend they had a purpose
in the world.
I refuse to be claimed.
Your plate is waiting.
We will snip fresh mint
into your tea.

INTIMACY, PART 3:

THE kitchen is a shared space, even if we live alone and cook only for ourselves. We share it with the bowl of plums sitting on the counter, with the stack of plates in the cupboard, with the often unacknowledged but still deeply felt presence and influence of those who have cooked for and with us in the past. And, of course, we share it with the living things that have given up their lives so that we may eat, animals and vegetables, and grains, legumes, and fruits.

We share it with our enormous, complicated world whose capricious events shape what we have in our cupboards and determine how well we will eat or even if we will eat at all. We share it with our own thoughts and predilections, with our habits and desires, with our moods. We share it with the kind of day we've just had and dragged in through the door with us as we put our backpack or briefcase or purse down on the counter and roll up our sleeves.

But, of course, the most significant way we share the kitchen is with other people—with our friends and families, colleagues and acquaintances, and even the occasional stranger. Cooking together, feeding each other, and being fed by each other is one of our deepest, oldest, and most powerful intimacies.

We mark every important event—every birth, death, and marriage—every transition, and every holiday with a feast of some sort. The foods we serve and eat reflect and express our culture and the sense of belonging that is so important to our happiness. It's how we express our caring, our love, our interest. Whether it's a family sitting down to their 4,857th dinner together or a young couple on their third date, eating together is as ancient as our humanity and as fundamental to it.

Sharing the World

SHARING the world is difficult. It doesn't take too much effort to explore the truth of this statement—just glance at your newsfeed or turn on the radio and the whole cacophonous mess will come pouring out. We humans are having a tough time of it, for the most part. We haven't quite mastered the art of sharing the world, and, as a result, we've been causing a lot of chaos and suffering, much of it completely unnecessary.

How do we begin to remedy this situation? Humans are complicated, and the world we've built reflects that complexity, so there's no one simple answer. Each one of us must take up this question within the context of our own lives and abilities. It is a universal dilemma that often calls for a very personal response.

Our first task is to slow down, pay attention, discover what's most important, and bring the truth of that into our lives. This kind of inquiry does not usually come forward in the restless push of our busyness, for what we will find there is often more distraction and busyness. It is revealed instead in the stillness that comes with pausing in the middle of the mayhem and finding our breath. This slowing down brings appreciation, and this appreciation allows for intimacy. And intimacy leads us to a clearer understanding of who we are and the world we live in.

And we cannot do this work alone. We share the world with others, and our biggest, most important undertaking right now is learning how to do that so we all have the chance to thrive. Every last one of us. How will we share the world? What do we need to understand in order to do that? What is the truth of this, and how can we live it?

Maybe our first gesture toward figuring this out is simple hospitality. Maybe we start by inviting people in to sit at the table, to have a meal, to drink mint tea. Some will be friends, some will be strangers, at least at first. Maybe some will be enemies, even. Some we will agree with and some not, but maybe, if we sit together long enough, we can start to unravel the knots of separation and fear.

This is a metaphor, of course. As much as I love the image of people in conflict gathered around a dinner table, I'm not so naive as to think this will actually happen. We tend to gather with those we know and love and while dinner table talk can spark and inspire, it obviously takes a lot more than a good dinner party to solve the world's problems. Still, it's helpful to consider hospitality as an initial response when encountering difficulty or something or someone new or strange.

What is hospitality? It's simply the notion of gracefully welcoming something in—usually a person or a group of people—but it can also be an idea or a situation. The basic stance of hospitality is friendliness and generosity and warmth. Its purpose is to bring comfort and ease to a situation so that there is relaxation and intimacy. When we're relaxed like this, when we have a sense of belonging, there is a willingness to be available and to be more open and tolerant.

The attitude of hospitality, if sincerely offered, has the power to transform and inspire. At the very least, it can de-escalate a difficult and tense situation and help set the stage for a more cooperative and nuanced communication. But it is also important to remember that hospitality belongs in our everyday lives as well, whether it's offering a visitor a seat and something to drink or being willing to remain open and available to a new idea.

So whether you're having friends over to dinner, or being confronted with something new or strange, or embarking on a quest to single-handedly change the world, it's helpful to have the notion of hospitality in mind. Even if the actual act of hospitality isn't possible, holding it as a basic tenant, as an overarching attitude, will bring the possibility of sharing the world to all that you do.

Is hospitality something important in your life? What do you invite in and what do you push away? What happens when you are welcoming? How are we going to take care of this wild, messy, mixed-up, deeply troubled, and stunningly beautiful world of ours?

Lingering

ONE of life's great pleasures is lingering at the table with folks you care about long after the main part of the meal is over. People are usually satiated and mellow at this point, perhaps even a little tipsy but not necessarily so. The table has become an ark of sorts, a kind of a refuge. It glows with good humor and ease, the candles sputtering in their holders, the mess in the kitchen most thoroughly ignored. This is a good time to bring out a nice bar of chocolate to pass around, a final shared pleasure as each person breaks off a square or two and hands the bar on to their neighbor.

Lingering also can happen over a weekend breakfast, perhaps in bed with the kids, perhaps on the couch with a good book, perhaps at the kitchen table with a new love and the coffeepot close at hand. Try it at a long lunch with an old friend, or a Sunday lunch with the family, or a backyard picnic as the sun travels across the sky and the shadows deepen. Even the ordinary week-night dinner table can be worthy of hanging around now and again.

Try to instill the habit of lingering in your life. Leave behind the urge to hurry on to the next thing and replace it with a hankering for the more settled, deeper conversations that develop when people commit to spending time together. Give someone the gift of saying "I have nowhere else I'd rather be than here with you." Shed the armor of busyness and distraction and see what happens when you choose to stay in one place for a while. Dawdle. Let the conversation meander. Enjoy the long, lingering present moment with good company and something delicious to share.

How to Be Ready for Anything

THERE was a time when having people over meant a lot of advance planning on my part. I cleaned, I shopped, I cooked, I added special decorating touches to the bathroom. Everything needed to be planned, polished, and perfected. From the light over the dining room table down to my toenails, it needed to shine. These days, I can still launch a fancy fete now and again, but more often than not, my entertaining is much simpler. And sloppier. And a lot more fun.

I live in the kind of place where it's easy for friends to just drop by. My apartment is on the ground floor with only an unlocked wooden gate and a screen door between me and whomever just happens to be in the neighborhood. My street usually has plenty of parking, and I'm not far from the post office, library, and other places where errand-running friends are passing through. Since I work from home, I tend to be around, and it's not unusual for me to hear a "yoo-hoo" followed by a knock on the door and the rattle of a paper bag from a nearby bakery.

A couple of years ago, this would have petrified me. Is the house clean? Are the dishes done? Do I have milk for tea or the makings of lunch? Did I brush my teeth yet? But now I'm simply happy for the company and welcome my friends in with a big hello and a hug. If my apartment is messy or the refrigerator is bare, we'll still make do. Besides, my friends know better than to expect a full spread if they've just dropped in. It's the company that matters; everything else is just window dressing.

Likewise, I'm much more apt to invite someone over on the spur of the moment. The most important question for me is "Do I want this conversation to continue?" and not "When did I last vacuum?" Again, the relationship and the mood of the moment is what's most important here. Of course, there are a few things I do to make this a little easier on myself. I make my bed every morning without fail, and usually I give my bathroom a quick 2-minute cleanup in the morning. In general, I never let my housecleaning go so far that I would be embarrassed to have people over.

I try to keep my pantry and refrigerator shelves stocked with things like olives, crackers, and other various nibbles, and there's usually a bottle of wine or lemonade or something to drink in the refrigerator. And even if there isn't, I can always offer a cup of tea. I remember once I invited a friend up for a snack and we sat at the kitchen table, dabbing almond butter and homemade plum preserves onto Ritz crackers. Fun and delicious!

In a pinch, I've served a few squares of nice chocolate on a napkin, or a glass of water with a slice of cucumber and a sprig of mint. Yesterday, there was only one peach in the fruit bowl, so I cut it in half, dolloped on some yogurt, and drizzled it with honey. I could have just as easily served it plain and simple in a pretty pedestaled bowl like they do at Chez Panisse.

The most important lesson for me has been to let go of this idea that everything has to be neat and perfect and in my control. The key to being ready for anything rests in a willingness to be available for anything, no matter what the circumstances. It's knowing what's most important (intimacy, friendship, connection) and allowing that to guide my actions, whether I'm opening the door to an unexpected knock or inviting the gang over for a spontaneous cocktail. The rule is simple: Never, never, never let a few dust bunnies get in the way of a really good conversation.

When Times Get Rough

IT'S sometimes hard to know what to do when bad things happen in the world. A restless energy can rise up within us, and we want to do something, but often there's nothing we can do, at least not immediately. It's impossible to sit on our hands and yet it's impossible not to.

Here's what I do when things get rough, when I'm sad or troubled or upset. It's a pretty simple formula: I go into the kitchen, I make something, and then I give it away to someone. I don't let it get too complicated: I pull some ingredients together from whatever is at hand and I make up a pot of soup, or a batch of cookies, or some bread. And then I give it to the first person I think of, usually someone who is close by, like a neighbor, or a coworker, or sometimes even my mail carrier.

I try to not make a big deal of it. This is not about forgetting the bad or fixing the problem at hand or putting on a happy face. It's more about injecting something positive into the mess, to countervail, to pull some of the weight away from the negative. It's about trying to find a deeper, more engaged way of working with the harsher aspects of having a human life. I like the small, intimate scale of this: a warm, alive human being handing over a paper sack full of biscotti or jars of warm soup and another warm, alive human being reaching out to take it. Very simple, very direct, immediate. No need to create a nonprofit here; no need to set up the card tables or web pages. Warm hand to warm hand is enough.

I like to think of it like a yoga pose that grounds one-half of the body in stillness, and then bends or leans or stretches or reaches the other half of the body away from the groundedness to find a new balance. Static and dynamic. Good and bad. Pain and pleasure. Find the balance that holds us steady and then, from that stability, turn toward the world and give.

The creative act of cooking, which helps to release and loosen the knots and tangles, followed by the connecting act of giving the results away is, for me, a powerful combination. When the situation is such that there's not much I can do, I find that I can indeed do something. And this something, as I said, doesn't necessarily fix the wrong, but it does help because it strengthens and nourishes the right.

As the world explodes and explodes and then explodes again, I hope you find ways of coping that are helpful and wholesome, ways that enable connection and strength and kinship. I hope you have the nourishment and fortitude to stand still in the middle of it and then, from that stillness, reach out and reach toward love. It is the only way.

Salsa Verde

Having a few sauces in your kitchen is the secret to always eating well and being prepared for the unexpected. Sauces go well over pasta, of course, and are a beautiful accompaniment to sliced meats and fish and can dress all matter of sautéed, grilled, or steamed vegetables. A few good sauces in your repertoire will assure that a delicious lunch or dinner is always only moments away. This makes it very possible to have an impromptu guest over for dinner or surprise your family with something wonderful in the middle of an ordinary week.

One of my favorite sauces is salsa verde, which comes in hundreds of variations that roughly divide into the European-influenced, which usually has parsley, capers, and anchovies, and the Mexican-influenced, which is made with cilantro and tomatillos. Both are excellent but my favorite lately is one made with parsley, chives, and tarragon. I made the anchovies optional here but please, give them a try even if you think you're anchovy adverse. They really do add an important depth and dimension. Feel free to experiment and create a salsa verde of your own!

½ cup finely chopped flat-leaf parsley

¼ cup finely chopped chives

2 tablespoons finely chopped tarragon

1 small shallot, finely chopped

1 tablespoon capers, drained and chopped

1 or 2 anchovy fillets (optional)

1 small clove garlic, finely chopped or microplaned

Zest from one lemon, finely chopped or microplaned

Large pinch of salt

A few grinds of pepper

½ cup olive oil, plus more if needed

COMBINE all ingredients in a medium bowl and stir. Taste for more salt. If it seems too dry, add more oil. Set aside to allow the flavors to blend. If you would like a more piquant sauce, add some lemon juice just before serving. The juice will darken the vibrant green color but the lemon will brighten the flavor of the sauce.

THIS sauce can also be made in the food processor. Start by pulsing the garlic, shallot, and (sort of but not really optional) anchovies until chopped. Then add the herbs (just roughly chopped, the processor will chop them finer), lemon zest, salt, and pepper and pulse until finely chopped. Add the olive oil, pulse again, and taste for seasoning.

Giving and Receiving
and Gratefulness

TO cook a meal for someone is to give them many gifts: the gift of your time and effort and resources; the gift of your regard for their health and well-being; the gifts of pleasure and sustenance and a place at the table. You are also giving the gift of your vulnerability: Here, eat this thing that I made just for you. Do you like it? Is it enough? Are you satisfied?

To be a guest is to receive these gifts and return them with your own gifts of presence and gratitude, of appreciation and enjoyment. It may seem like you are doing the bulk of the receiving but actually all the roles (giver, receiver, and gift, too) are not fixed positions but in a dynamic interplay together, a kind of call and response.

It is nearly impossible to separate the acts of giving and receiving, for when we truly receive something, that very act of receiving is automatically transformed into a gift that's given back to the giver. And when we are on the giving end, we receive the gift of that response—hopefully, delight and appreciation but, of course, not always. There is pleasure in giving and it, too, is part of the gift itself.

So it's kind of hard to picture giving and receiving as two separate activities or roles to play. Or to think of receiving as being the passive, accepting stance and giving as being the active, granting one. It's really just too messy and complex to be seen this simplistically. To truly receive a gift, to be open to it, accepting of it, to receive it fully with grace and appreciation is a very dynamic position to be in. And to give a gift may seem powerful (think of the words associated with giving: *bestow, provide, permit*) but, in fact, it has many vulnerabilities. To give something is to risk rejection. You can miss the mark and give something inappropriate or unappreciated.

And in the middle of it all is gratefulness—the act of being aware of this dynamic equation, seeing its ever-present power in our lives, and feeling the joy that accompanies it. Both giver and receiver are expressing gratitude, and this gratefulness is a very powerful place to inhabit. To say thank-you when you are fully aware of what you have received is to be humbled and enlivened by both the gift and the receiving of it.

When thinking about giving and receiving and gratitude, it's important to not fall into the trap of indebtedness and quid pro quo. It's not about diligently keeping track of whose turn it is and doing things just for payback. It's more about allowing the power and energy of giving and receiving to be a conscious force in your life. It is the natural outcome of attention, for with attention comes appreciation. When you open up a little and find appreciation, you cannot help but want to give something over to it, to sustain it. As you receive the joy, you will automatically return the joy. This is a good equation, a nice dance move, to have active in your life. It's worth trying out, experimenting with. Start with gratitude and see what happens.

Unexpected Gifts from the Kitchen

ONE of the best kinds of gifts to receive (and to give!) is the unexpected gift: the one that's given outside of the constraints of obligation and expectation or that is attached to a holiday or specific celebration but arises spontaneously out of appreciation and generosity and the impulse to connect. These gifts do not have to be elaborate. In fact, the smaller and simpler, the better— it's often not so much the object given but the act of giving that creates an opportunity for pleasure and intimacy.

The kitchen provides us with lots of good giving material, making it easy to practice spontaneous gift-giving without a lot of fuss and bother. It's important to not be too concerned with perfection here—it's not necessary for your gift to be fancy or beribboned or even neat and tidy. Some of my favorite kitchen gifts came embellished with just a sticky thumbprint and a piece of masking tape for a label. Or were pleasantly wonky in shape or unique in flavor or very specific to the giver: so-and-so's famous crabapple chutney or my father's jars of applesauce tucked into my laundry basket when I was home visiting from college.

That said, I do tend to wash out and save pretty jars and bottles and stash them under my kitchen sink for exactly this purpose. I also have a tin of sticky labels and a fat black pen for marking the jars with their contents and the date, which is an important thing to do.

What to give? Baked goods are an obvious choice: a plate of cookies or scones, a slice of pie (or a whole pie!), or a loaf of bread are all classic gifts from your oven. A homemade jar of jam or preserves from your stash is also good, although the popularity of home canning has created a bit of an eye-rolling glut these days. Other possibilities are:

- A mason jar full of soup or homemade stock
- Preserved lemons (be sure to give instructions on how to use them)
- A container of tomato sauce for the freezer
- A jar of lemon or lime curd
- Dried fruits from your tree—or fresh ones, too, when in season
- Boozy beverages like vin d'orange or your home-brewed beer

- A few scoops from a jar of a new spice you just discovered
- A handful of herbs from your garden or some veg from your farm box (as long as you're not trying to fob off something undesired—no foot-long zucchini!)

When to give? Whenever the mood strikes! If you're not usually inclined to spontaneity or gift-giving, then you can prompt yourself until the habit takes hold. Having a shelf or a corner of a shelf devoted to potential kitchen gifts helps, but remember, this isn't about feeling pressured or obligated. It's about discovering and encouraging your capacity to give and receive, to whatever degree works for you.

So the next time you bake some bread, make an extra loaf for your neighbor. When it comes out of the oven, wrap it up in a brown paper bag, throw on a sweater, and walk it on over, the loaf still a little warm from the oven, the crust popping and crackling in the cool air. It may be a humble loaf, but it's also a treasure, an unexpected delight to be shared and enjoyed.

Meal Blessings

SOME people never say grace, and for others, it's a daily ritual, as much a part of the meal as the food itself. Or for some, it happens only on special occasions like Thanksgiving or at dinner when the whole family is gathered around the table.

Why do we say meal blessings? Maybe it's because of tradition, or religious mandate, or even genuine gratitude. Or perhaps it's just a habit or an instinct. Sometimes, it's a desire to connect, or to teach children to value and appreciate their food. And then there are the moments when everyone is gathered together and the simple act of saying "thank you" seems appropriate.

Sometimes, meal blessings are about acknowledging just how tentative and precious life is and that we cannot do it alone. They can be teachings of respect and interconnectedness, or an acknowledgment of labor. Or for some, there's the desire to stop and focus attention on receiving what's been given and the many forms of nourishment that this brings.

I imagine that food blessings originated way, way

back when food was a precious thing and having food in your bowl was not taken casually. Maybe we were a little closer to the fact that something had to give up its life in order for us to be fed. We were also a little closer to the physicality of obtaining food, that hunting and gathering as well as planting and harvesting are hard work and not always successful.

I know food security is not an issue for many people, or at least it's not something we think much about. It's difficult to understand scarcity when we walk into any one of the many large grocery chains in any city and are confronted with an enormous store of food, from those piles of apples and tomatoes to that never-ending cereal aisle. This might be a good place to say a blessing, don't you think? Or even just to pause a moment and take in the overwhelming abundance that is before you. It is actually rather astonishing.

If you're not inclined to stop dead in your tracks in the middle of your local grocery store, then try pausing right now to consider all the things that needed to go right for food to be available. To start: weather, good farming practices, good soil, the good health and strength of the farmer and the crew. A functioning infrastructure of roads and rails to get the food to your store. More labor to receive and stock and check out your food, more infrastructure to get it home and stored properly. That this enormous chain of effort and luck and maintenance is successful nearly each and every day is a true marvel.

I recommend being profligate with your gratitude and blessings. Bestow them upon farm fields as well as your backyard garden. Lemonade stands and roadside farm stands with honor boxes and bake sales are worthy of them, too. Potlucks and church suppers and TV dinners, even that drive-thru burger: Whenever there is nourishment, there's an opportunity to give thanks.

Many people assume that saying grace or a meal blessing is only for the religious but that's not necessarily so. If the traditional form of a blessing (bowed heads, folded hands) is not for you, there are many other ways to express your gratitude. A moment of stillness and silence before picking up your fork, a poem, a simple "thank you" spoken out loud—there are countless way to notice and appreciate the astonishing plenty that supports, nourishes, and makes it possible for us to be here.

Love and Time

**I want to love the things as no one has
thought to love them, until they're
worthy of you and real.**

—Rainer Maria Rilke

TAKE these turnips, for example, sitting there on my
cutting board, their lush green tops posing as many
questions as the cheerful white globes themselves. What
to do with them? Raw or cooked? Whole or chopped?
Simply roasted or something more elaborate? Glazed?
Wilted? Steamed? Pickled? Served with something or
separately?

The near infinite possibilities of raw ingredients are
limited only by a cook's imagination. With raw ingredients, we begin at the beginning and all the decisions are
ours. This can be thrilling or daunting, depending on
our skills and confidence and how much we enjoy a
challenge. All of the decisions are ours, and the responsibility and the credit as well.

The immediate challenge of raw ingredients is time.

While a can of creamed corn can sit on a pantry shelf for months (years?), an ear of corn needs attending to pronto or much of what is good about it will be lost. Time quite simply cannot be ignored, or not for long. Nor can we ignore the broader sweep of the seasons or the influence of the current weather. Or how long it takes to coax the rawness from an ingredient into something more complex and desirable—or not, of course. One of the possible decisions is to do very little, or nothing at all.

The immediacy and tension of this race with time creates an intimacy that, to me at least, is more than just pleasant: It is necessary. This is how we love the things as no one has thought to love them. This is how we lean in closer, look deeper, and discover what lies hidden within. We can survive on the safe and distant diet of canned goods and processed foods but it will be only that, a survival. Far, far better is to take the risky path with something that is equally invested in time as we are, equally perishable and equally weighted with potential.

Of course, there are evenings when the weary cook enters the kitchen with barely enough energy to lift a can opener, and, in these moments, whatever it is she eats will mostly be about convenience. But hopefully, this is a rare occurrence. Hopefully, we can learn to create the balance in our lives that shows us what to love and appreciate and how to love it like no other. To be engaged with and appreciative of something—let's say a handful of turnips—is to be, in that moment at least, worthy of it and real.

Sautéed Tiny Turnips with Their Greens
Serves 4

—●

Tokyo turnips are beautiful, creamy white turnips.
They are often sold golf-ball size with their greens
still attached. If you can't find them, try using
regular turnips (one or two medium-size will do) and
sub in a small bunch of kale for the greens. This is a
simple dish that comes together quickly. It makes
a nice side or even an elegant first course if plated
individually. If you want to make it vegan,
use olive oil instead of butter.

The mixture of tahini and lemon is alchemical.
It's what makes hummus so delicious, and it works
beautifully here with the bitter-into-sweet funkiness
of the turnips. The tahini likes to seize up when the
lemon juice is added but a few splashes of water
should help to create a clingy sauce.

Marash pepper comes from Turkey. It has a gorgeous brick-red color and an earthy, somewhat mellow heat. You can find it in well-stocked spice shops and specialty grocery stores and online. It's worth seeking out but if you can't find it, use a pinch of your favorite hot pepper instead (or you can just skip it).

2 bunches small Tokyo turnips, with their greens

1 tablespoon freshly squeezed lemon juice

2 tablespoons tahini

2 tablespoons butter

Big pinch of salt

1 small clove garlic, finely minced or microplaned

1 teaspoon black sesame seeds, for garnish

Pinch of Marash pepper, for garnish

USING a sharp knife, trim the greens from the turnips, leaving a small ⅛-inch bit of stem on the bulbs. Cut most of the stem away from the leafy greens and discard. Keeping them separate, wash the turnips and greens in lots of cold water and drain. Repeat the washing step if the turnips are very sandy or dirty. Cut the turnips in half, or into quarters if especially large.

MIX the lemon juice and tahini in a small bowl. It may stiffen, which is okay for now. Set aside.

SAUTÉED TINY TURNIPS WITH THEIR GREENS

MELT the butter in a medium skillet over medium heat. Add the turnips, cut side down and in a single layer, if possible, along with a good splash of water and the salt. Cover and simmer until the turnips begin to brown and the water has almost evaporated. Remove the cover, raise the heat, and shake the pan so the turnips begin to brown a little on their other sides.

ADD the turnip greens and the garlic to the turnips. It's nice if the greens have a little water still clinging to them, which will steam and help them cook, or add a small splash of water. Continue to shake the pan or toss with tongs until the greens wilt and become soft. Remove from the heat.

USING tongs, remove the turnips (leaving the greens in the pan) and put them in a bowl. Cover to keep warm. Return the pan to the heat and add the lemon and tahini mixture. Toss to coat, adding a splash of water, as needed, so that the mixture is creamy. Taste for salt.

TO serve, arrange the leaves in a rough nest on a shallow platter. Tumble on the turnips, mounding them slightly in the center. Sprinkle with the sesame seeds and pepper and serve immediately.

We're Never the Same

AS cooks, we deal with the spare and simple truth that all things are in a constant state of change on a daily basis.

The avocado ripening on the counter, the cheese aging in the refrigerator, the onions going from raw to cooked in the sputtering fat of a frying pan. Cabbages into sauerkraut, wheat and yeast and salt into a loaf of bread. Everywhere and all the time, we are working with change. All day long, we monitor and encourage (and discourage) and are impacted by this act of transformation.

We work with the changing seasons, too. Kale grows sweeter in the colder months, peaches concentrate their sugar and flavor when the summer grows hot and the rains stop. I remember as a child growing up in Wisconsin that the milk tasted different in the winter when the cows were taken off of grass and switched to their winter feed. And, of course, our cravings change, too, as we reach for simple, cool food in summer and richer and heavier dishes in winter.

What we often forget is that this goes for people as well. It's easier, and often safer, to fix a person in our minds, boxing them into our judgments and observations and not allowing them to be any different. So-and-so is the flighty one and will never make anything of herself; Mr. Businessman over there has no heart and cannot be trusted. Maybe we're too busy, maybe we're just lazy, or maybe it simply never occurs to us that people are complex and multilayered and they, like everything, are never unchanging.

It's more complicated and riskier for us to meet a person fresh each time we see them. We humans like to know what we're dealing with, and so it's convenient for us to hold others to our impressions of them, even if those impressions are incomplete or biased. This limits us, it limits them, and it limits our relationship and the possibilities it can bring. It's helpful, then, to be curious, especially with people we think we know or understand. Experiment with this. Try seeing someone you know as if they're brand new to you. Don't assume. Look for clues that they may be more than your opinion of them, that they might have another side, another layer beyond the limits you've imposed.

I have a friend who is generally considered to be a difficult person. He's moody, quick to anger, and always finds the negative in situations. But for some reason, those qualities don't bother me. I can also see that he is generous and loyal, and that he has a quick and playful wit that often makes me laugh. When I'm with him, I see him and treat him as this loyal and playful person. And in doing so, I believe he becomes more of that part of himself. The other stuff doesn't go away, it's true, but the more positive stuff seems to come forward.

There are no guarantees that a mean ol' cuss will be any different today than he was yesterday. But it's always worthwhile to find out, to poke around a little and see if something bright and beautiful is lurking in the messy and difficult stuff. I know that I would feel terrible if someone met me at my worst moment and then always saw me as that person. Wouldn't you?

Circling back to the kitchen, this is how we work with our ingredients, too. We expect the dandelion greens to be bitter, but how bitter? Will they be as bitter as the last bunch? How much honey should I add this time? Taste first and see and then adjust accordingly. Some days it will just be a drop or two, other days we may need to measure out something more substantial.

Working in the kitchen has taught me a lot about working with the changing nature of things. It has taught me how to yield to it and accept it, and it has also taught me how to encourage it and make it work for me. Knowing when to do one or the other is truly the work of a wise person and, to be frank, is often beyond my capacity. But I keep at it, trying to greet each thing (each ingredient, each person, each moment, each situation) as if it were brand new, balancing my need for safety with a willingness to be surprised and delighted. Can I see and appreciate and accept what is offered, just as it is, and see and appreciate and accept it when it changes?

No small thing, this.

Alone, Too

IN my life, there have been two kinds of kitchens. The first is the social kitchen, where friends or family gather to cook and talk and dance and generally make merry. These are boisterous places, where people are always bumping into one another and spilling drinks and making glorious messes. I love this wild, often slightly out-of-control way of being in the kitchen and the beautiful sense of belonging it creates.

But I also love the silent kitchen where it's just me, a pile of vegetables, and my sharpest knife. The sounds and smells of cooking fill the room, and my mind can completely engage with the task at hand. Full concentration, full immersion. In Zen, it is said that nirvana is doing one thing completely, seeing one thing completely through to the end. If that's true, then cooking offers many excellent opportunities for experiencing nirvana.

Sometimes, I stay completely silent, just the sound of my knife chopping or the olive oil sizzling, occasionally accompanied by the refrigerator's hum or a flock of scolding ravens in the tree outside of my window. And sometimes, of course, there's music to inspire and encourage or an audiobook to keep me company. But truthfully, I find even that can be too distracting so more often than not, I keep to the silence.

It's rare to have the chance to be alone in this hyper-connected world, so it may take some effort to create silent, solitary time in the kitchen. But I urge you to make that effort now and then. Send your roommates or family away, haul out an engaging and slightly complicated recipe, and do nothing but cook. What comes forth when there is nothing mediating your experience but the task at hand? Is being alone with your thoughts refreshing or scary? Boring or fascinating? What does kitchen nirvana feel like?

Unambitious

IT'S important to remember that our cooking doesn't always have to be fabulous; it doesn't always have to be perfect, or showcase the latest, most expensive ingredient. Sometimes, a dinner consisting of a simple unambitious plate of spaghetti with a decent red sauce and a nice green salad is good enough. In fact, it is perfect. Perfect for every day and perfect for company, too.

Not surprisingly, we can sometimes let our ego get the best of us in the kitchen, and it becomes a place where we push and strive and battle as if dinner were some kind of sporting event that one must dominate at all costs. Achievement, excellence, mastery, and ambition are highly valued in our culture, but they can sometimes obscure the more subtle treasures like connection, intimacy, and fellowship. In reaching for the stars, we can overlook the more humble but incredibly delicious and nourishing offerings right here at our feet.

So if you want to be a great cook and, even more important, a great friend and host, learn to make the best spaghetti Bolognese you can. Or the best chickpea curry or the best grilled cheese sandwich or tossed salad. Go for simple, honest, straightforward food served up to nourish and delight. The idea is not to impress but to put people at ease, to gratify them with something delicious, and to let them know that their company is the most important thing at the table. Everything else is just extra.

Bolognese Sauce
Makes enough for 1 pound of pasta; serves 4 to 6

This hearty meat sauce is an Italian classic, and there are about as many recipes for it as there are people who cook it. This is my favorite. Be sure to slice the carrots thinly so that they cook quickly and almost disappear into the sauce. I like to use whole milk but don't sweat it if you only have 1% or 2% in the house.

This Bolognese contains bacon, which is unconventional. I suppose if you have pancetta, you could use some of that but the truth is, most folks have better luck finding bacon. It adds just the right notes of smoky meatiness, so be sure to use it.

To serve, cook the pasta (I prefer a hearty long noodle like fettuccini or bucatini, which looks like spaghetti but is hollow in the middle) and save a cup of water before draining. Transfer the cooked pasta immediately to the pan with the sauce and toss, adding splashes of the pasta water to loosen the sauce, as needed.

2 strips smoked bacon

8 ounces button mushrooms, cleaned and coarsely chopped

Olive oil, as needed

1 onion, chopped

1 large carrot, very thinly sliced

¾ pound ground beef

¼ pound ground pork

2 cloves garlic, chopped

1 (28-ounce) can whole tomatoes

¾ cup whole milk

1 teaspoon dried thyme

Salt and pepper

PLACE a large skillet over medium heat, add the bacon, and fry until crisp. Remove the bacon from the pan and set aside.

ADD the mushrooms to the bacon fat, drizzling in a little oil if the pan is too dry. Cook the mushrooms until they start to brown, stirring occasionally, 3 to 5 minutes. Stir in the onion and carrot and cook until the onion is translucent, lowering the heat a little, if needed. Add the ground beef and pork, and cook, stirring, until the meat begins to brown.

CRUMBLE the bacon and stir it into the pan along with the garlic. Add the tomatoes along with their juices, breaking them up with a spoon. Cook a few minutes longer then add the milk, thyme, a big pinch of salt, and several grinds of pepper. Simmer for 30 minutes, or until the sauce thickens.

SERVE on your pasta of choice, garnished with lots of freshly grated Parmesan on top.

THIS recipe is easily doubled—you may need to switch to a Dutch oven to hold everything—and can be frozen for up to 6 months.

The Best Way to Learn
How to Cook

IN these modern times, we often learn how to cook—
how to prepare a recipe, perform a technique—through
online searches and TV shows. This instantaneous finding of information is nothing short of miraculous and
one I indulge in frequently. So it's not my intention to
dismiss the vast, ever-changing cookbook of the Internet when I say that the best way to learn how to cook is
from another human being. A live one who is right
there beside you.

The reason for this is that cooking, at its most fundamental, is responding to the causes and conditions of
the present moment. A cookbook or video or recipe can
offer broad guidelines but a real live person can help you
navigate those more subtle movements and decisions
and understandings needed in order to cook well. In the
middle of making a Bolognese, they can tell you about
which garlic clove is best to use and why. They can tell
you that the sauce might need a stir now and that actually a splash of water might be good right now. They

can remind you to smell and taste and ask you if you think fresh basil is better than dried at this point. When you learn from a person, cooking becomes a conversation, not just a set of directions.

This friend or relative or neighbor may also challenge you in ways you might not challenge yourself, encouraging you to take on something bigger or to go in a direction you would have never considered on your own. The poet and essayist Wendell Berry says that "It is not from ourselves that we learn to be better than we are." Inviting another person into your kitchen means you have remained teachable, that you are not done learning, that you have the wisdom to understand that you will never know it all. It means you believe in possibilities and the freedom they bring.

Of course, it's not always possible for us to learn from another person (page 229) but if the opportunity arises, don't hesitate. Ask the friend who makes that killer chocolate cake if she wouldn't mind showing you how, take a cooking class, volunteer in a kitchen where real cooking is done. Hang out with your grandma and learn her secrets before it's too late. Learn from a real, breathing, thinking, responding person.

This is warm-hand-to-warm-hand transmission, which is more than just technique-building and improvement. It's about the intimacies and lessons learned from being human with another human. Ten thousand words can be said in a glance, ten million moments of being alive can be shared in a single touch, a simple word. Don't miss the chance to know someone in this way, to share yourself with someone in this way. Your cooking, if not your whole life, will be the better for it.

Kitchen Ancestors and Other Influences

WHILE the best way to learn how to cook is from a real person, we don't always have one at our side when we need one. Sometimes, we have to learn from books or TV or the Internet, and, of course, there is nothing wrong with that. There are many excellent cooking teachers out there whom you can only get to know through their books or TV appearances or Web sites. So go on and get to know them!

Becoming a devotee of a cookbook author or chef, learning their particular ways and methods and recipes, trusting their voice and palate and learning, is a wonderful way to deepen your kitchen skills. I have several friends (and myself included) who swear by Julia Child, Deborah Madison, or Nigel Slater and consult their cookbooks regularly, if not daily. They tell me about hearing their voices in their heads whenever they make their recipes or use their techniques and I know exactly what they mean.

I like to think of these influences as kitchen ancestors

and put them up there with my real kitchen ancestors—my mother and father, and my maternal grandfather. I love having their companionship in the kitchen and their voices in my head when I'm taking on one of their recipes. I can feel them lean over my shoulder and say, "Maybe it needs a touch more salt" or "Let the tomato paste caramelize a little—it will add more flavor," and I am immediately grateful for what they have so generously shared.

And that is the true seasoning, the final touch, to any meal: generosity and gratitude—knowing what you have been given and learning how to give it back.

Hiding Out in the Kitchen

THE kitchen is a great place to hide, which is a good thing because sometimes hiding is the best response when life gets overwhelming. This is particularly true when we share our lives closely with other people (spouse, partner, kids, roommates). A wise person knows when it's time to back off and disappear for a while, when all we need is some time alone to take a few deep breaths and find our feet again.

But most adults have a hard time disappearing. We have responsibilities and people who are counting on us. We have made promises, we have obligations, we have goals and ambitions and an image of ourselves that somehow includes "superhero" spelled out in glitter on our backs. So when it comes time to disappear, we have to figure out a way to do that so that it doesn't look like we've actually disappeared. This is where the kitchen can help.

The kitchen gives you a good cover story. It makes it look like you're busy and doing something (which of course you are), but what's really happening is that you have stepped away from the crowd, away from the fra-cas, and have bought yourself some time alone. It might only be for 5 minutes (because Lord knows eventually some of that fracas is going to follow you right in) but still, there will be a moment or two to shake off some stress and tension. It's even possible to train people to leave you alone while you're cooking, especially if they understand that this is the price they need to pay for enjoying dinner later on.

So don't worry or hesitate if you find yourself want-ing to disappear into the kitchen. It truly can be a place of refuge, where you can ratchet down the drama of a wild day into the simple, even soothing, tasks of chop-ping and peeling and stirring. Try using the motion of bending down to put a pan of lasagna into the oven as an excuse to do a few deep, bendy stretches. Feel your body uncoil and your mind empty out all the useless chatter and concerns and distractions it has been har-boring. Open up. Breathe. Discover yourself again in the kitchen.

On Counting What Is Precious

IN famine, the number of dried beans in the cupboard; in abundance, piles of chicken bones and empty wine bottles. In sorrow, so many tears that they oversalt the soup; in happiness, the number of place settings at a wedding feast. In middle age, candles on the cake; in youth, the frosting roses. In celebration, bubbles in a champagne glass; in mourning, the number of bites taken from a sandwich, delivered to your door draped in a napkin (none).

In planting, the number of seeds and rows; in harvest, the bushels of fruits and vegetables. In sickness, the spoonfuls of weak broth barely managed to be swallowed; in health, the number of courses at the fancy bistro plus a little nightcap at the tavern down the street. In winter, three puffs of breath blown on the surface of hot chocolate; in summer, five ice cubes in the tall glass of lemonade.

In trust, everything; in suspicion, nothing.

In babyhood, the number of tiny spoons of stewed carrots that actually make it into the mouth; in old age, the number of tiny spoons of stewed carrots that actually make it into the mouth mixed with the memories of parties and holidays and feasts beyond compare. In life, the uncountable stream of nourishment that sustains, enlivens, entertains, celebrates; in death, well, we can't know that yet.

In good times, we grow distracted and we forget to count; in bad times, we can only remember and wish we had.

Cooking Together

THERE are two types of people in the world: those that like to cook with others and those that prefer to cook alone. I understand wanting to cook alone: You have more control and fewer distractions. In many ways, being alone in the kitchen is much easier than navigating another person who may have different rhythms or very set ideas about how things are done, or who ends up needing more help than they give. Or maybe you don't mind the extra people but your current kitchen is just too small to handle more than one person. There are lots of good reasons to find yourself in the kitchen, alone.

That said, there is something quite wonderful that happens when we cook together, when we share the pleasures of the kitchen: the heady scents and little tastes, the moments of triumph when something turns out really well (and the commiseration when it doesn't), and, of course, the second opinion—sometimes helpful, sometimes not so much. There's the quiet chatter and intimacy that develops as many hands work together on a big project. And there's working together in silence, too, heads bent over the task at hand, no need for words to fill the space for it is already full enough with ease and companionship.

The most difficult thing about cooking together is avoiding stepping on each other's toes. This is not that hard to do if you agree on one simple thing on the onset: who is in charge. Some people need to be the boss, and this role can feel especially strong if it's their kitchen or their menu. If this dynamic is present, don't fight it. Show up and say: "What can I do? How can I help?" And be willing to take orders, to do what needs to be done. In some ways, it's a bit of a relief to not run the show for a while, to let someone else carry the burden of the meal. If this is impossible for you, then ask to take on one dish so that you have something to direct all your micromanaging energy into. The same goes if someone is trying to take over your kitchen—give them one dish to work on, something complicated enough to keep them occupied.

But still, the most important thing to cultivate when cooking together is an attitude of openness and availability. We all have our notions of how things should be done, and we're often rather partial to them. Sometimes, these ideas and preferences are helpful but mostly it's better to keep our mouths shut. Showing up and saying to someone "What can I do?" and then doing it without a lot of fuss and bother is a great gift, both in or out of the kitchen.

Finally, a word of advice about literally stepping on toes. There's an old restaurant trick where the custom is to say "behind you" when maneuvering through the kitchen and to sometimes gently touch the person on their shoulder to let them know you are there. This, and the practice of walking with your knife so that it is pointed to the ground, the blade slightly pressed up against your thigh, will help keep everyone safe and happy!

Cake and the Unexpected Guest

ONE of the pleasures of life is spontaneity, a quality that is often lacking these days as we fill our calendars with a schedule more tightly packed and regulated than an Olympic athlete in training. But a spontaneous invitation to come over for a cup of tea or to pop in on a friend just because you're in the neighborhood is a real delight and one we should partake in more often.

The best way to encourage spontaneity is to also encourage its opposite: preparation. If you want to be the kind of person who enjoys an impromptu gathering, then stock your kitchen with things that make it easy. There are many ways to do this but one of my favorites is to keep a simple, unfrosted, single layer cake on hand. I use any favorite cake recipe—carrot cake, walnut cake, chocolate cake, lemon cake—and bake it off in two round 8- or 9-inch layers. When cool, one layer is frozen for future use and the other is kept in an airtight container, where it can last up to a week.

To serve, simply cut a wedge of cake, put it on a nice

plate, and dust it with powdered sugar. It is excellent with a cup of strong coffee or tea or even a small glass of sherry or vin santo. If the cake is a few days old, you may want to freshen it up with a layer of jam or a drizzle of warm honey. This simple cake is also a nice way to treat yourself to a little after-dinner sweet without going overboard with something heavier or frosted.

Allowing for unplanned moments is an important element in a happy, satisfied life. We need to open doors, wander pathways, and go off-schedule every now and then in order to invite the unexpected into our lives. In doing so, we discover our capacity for flexibility and trust, and our lives are richer for the addition of experiences and thoughts and discoveries found outside of our usual boundaries.

The best news is, you don't need to travel to far-flung exotic places to experience this. Just be more spontaneous, change your routine, open up unknown doors in your day-to-day life. Bake up a single layer cake and invite the world over for a cup of tea.

My Mother's Spice Cake
Makes two 8-inch round layers

·—

My mother serves this with a classic cream cheese
frosting but it is just as delicious, or maybe even more
so, served plain with a sprinkle of powdered sugar.
People who say they don't like cake tend to like this one.

1½ sticks unsalted butter, softened, plus more for pans

Flour, for pans

2½ cups flour

1 teaspoon baking powder

½ teaspoon baking soda

½ teaspoon ground cinnamon

½ teaspoon ground cardamom

½ teaspoon ground ginger

½ teaspoon freshly grated nutmeg

¼ teaspoon ground cloves

½ teaspoon salt

1 cup packed brown sugar

½ cup sugar

3 large eggs

1 teaspoon pure vanilla extract

1 cup sour cream

PREHEAT the oven to 350°F. Butter and flour two 8" × 2" round cake pans.

IN a medium bowl, whisk the flour, baking powder, baking soda, cinnamon, cardamom, ginger, nutmeg, cloves, and salt so that everything is incorporated.

IN a large bowl or using a stand mixer fitted with a paddle, beat the butter, brown sugar, and sugar until fluffy, scraping the bowl, as needed. Add the eggs, one at a time, beating well after each addition, followed by the vanilla and the sour cream.

ADD in the flour mixture, beating until just incorporated, scraping down the sides of the bowl, as needed.

POUR the batter into the prepared pans, dividing evenly. Bake for 30 to 35 minutes, or until the cakes begin to pull away from the sides and the middle springs back when lightly touched. Cool for 10 minutes, then invert each layer onto a rack and let cool completely.

WRAP one cake in double layers of plastic wrap or waxed paper and freeze for up to 3 months. Be sure to label it with the date and contents. Wrap the other layer in waxed paper and store in an airtight tin for up to a week. It will improve with age.

SERVE in wedges on a plate. If you're feeling fancy, top with softly whipped, lightly sweetened cream. Extra-fancy plus: Add some finely chopped candied ginger to the whipped cream. It really is most delicious served plain, though, with the powdered sugar and a cup of strong hot coffee and hopefully someone wonderful to share it with.

Finding Yourself in the Kitchen with Children

COOKING with children is a subject that deserves its own book, so to touch on it lightly here seems insufficient. Still, I didn't want to ignore this sometimes delightful and sometimes challenging situation completely. Children are very curious beings, and the kitchen often fascinates them. They love food, they love to get their hands dirty, and they like to be a part of things. If your child feels this way, then take advantage of their natural affinity for cooking and build yourself your own wee sous chef!

Depending on their age, a child's motor skills may be somewhat wobbly and their attention spans fleeting, but they still have much to offer; the sooner you get them started, the quicker they will become active, talented, engaged cooks. I have seen this happen over and over again and cannot recommend it enough.

Start small and simple. Give them their own apron, an appropriately-sized knife, and a stool to stand on. Stay close, teach them safety, and allow their curiosity to flourish. One fun project is to engage your child with the whole meal, from planning, shopping (or harvesting), prepping, cooking, and serving to the final cleanup. Of course, they won't be doing all the work but to have them participate at each stage is an important learning opportunity for them and makes it possible for them to claim the meal as their own, which they will love to do.

Or consider learning a specific skill with your child, such as bread-baking. When I was little, both my grandfather and father were bread bakers and I would often find great joy in assisting them. I even remember the little bread loaf pan my grandfather bought just for me and the way the cinnamon and sugar smelled when my dad and I would roll it into the bread dough—the yeasty tang tempered by sweet sugar and rich, warm cinnamon.

Time spent with your child in the kitchen is sure to be an adventure for you both but I doubt it will be time regretted. In fact, I would say that if you don't have a child of your own, go out and "borrow" one, for they bring a delightfully fresh energy to the tasks at hand.

Patience with People

IT'S all well and good to practice patience with the ingredients and processes in our kitchen. A few rough moments with an undercooked chicken, and we're well on our way to learning the hard lesson that there's no rushing certain situations, that things simply cannot be done until they are done. But being patient with another human being and the elaborate tangle of their expectations and desires and predilections, now that's a much more complex event.

It's the intimacy of the kitchen that brings us right up against the edges of our patience. Intimacy means we are allowing something in, and that allowing means we're going to get the whole thing, the real deal: the good, the bad, and the difficult. Working with people underfoot or feeding someone who doesn't appreciate your efforts or whose demands seem unfair can bring about great frustration and disappointment. The question is: Now what? In other words, okay, this is getting to be a tough situation, so what is workable here? Patience is the first step toward finding the answer to that question.

When we are patient with a person, we aren't pushing them away, we are in fact asking them to move in closer. This can be difficult, especially when aversion is present, but that closeness is what will lead us toward a workable solution. It will allow us to see what's on the other side of the difficulty. It might even be something bright and beautiful. At the very least, it won't be nearly as bad as the suffering of our distance and dissatisfaction.

There are no simple solutions to the troubles that come up between people, but if we want intimacy, if we want closeness, if we want a lasting solution to a difficulty, then we're going to need to find patience. Patience is a practice, as it is not something that always arises easily. We often need to dig deep to find it and to work on it every day. But without it, it is impossible to dance the sometimes difficult, sometimes effortless, always exquisite dance of intimacy.

Terrible, Horrible,
No Good Comparisons

I once had a neighbor spontaneously ask me over to dinner on a quiet midweek evening. She didn't have much in the house, just a few basic items from Trader Joe's and some fixings for a salad. Halfway through our meal, she confessed that she almost didn't ask me, given the meager offerings of her pantry. "You're such a food person," she said, "you must make the most fabulous dinners. How can this possibly compare?"

The answer is that when it comes to cooking and feeding others, it's never about comparing. Ever.

The most tragic ending I can think of for my friend's little story would be if she would have given in to her critical thoughts and never invited me over. We would have missed out on each other's company, on the fine and pleasant conversation we had, on our chance to discover that we both had the same old apple-shaped cookie jar on our kitchen shelf. I would have missed browsing her wonderful book collection and catching sweet glimpses of her shy kitten and, of course, her perfectly wonderful meal. It was a lovely night, food included, and it almost didn't happen.

Moral of the story: Being stuck in comparing yourself and your efforts is a terrible, horrible, no good way to spend a life. It will prevent you from accomplishing anything worthwhile. It will prevent you from having meaningful relationships. It will prevent you from having fun. Don't do it!

Of course, it's nearly impossible to avoid comparison altogether. It seems to be human nature to measure ourselves against others or even our own previous efforts. We can certainly learn and grow from what we discover when we do that, but, if we linger too long, if we get stuck there or let it color our own accomplishments, then all is lost. Let the work of others inspire and motivate you, but, if you begin to feel the sticky, anxious claw of comparison, then pause, take a deep breath, and reset the channel.

Easier said than done, of course. But we have to try. Sometimes, this means clamping down rather hard on negative thinking, for comparison can be a tough habit to break. Sometimes, we even have to push through our critical opinions and offer up our best effort with love and good cheer and just hope for the best. Anyone worth knowing and loving will be more interested in your company than nitpicking about the food, so don't worry. Whatever you bring to the table will be just fine, it will be enough, it will be delicious without compare.

Taking Refuge

SOMETIMES, when life gets too full of stress and obligation and disappointments, I lock my door, bury my cell phone under the bed pillows, and start chopping carrots.

When all the carrots are chopped, I move to onions.

When the onions are done, I push a few cloves of garlic under my knife.

Usually, by the time the garlic's done, I'm more relaxed, present, and maybe even a little happy.

It's time to move on to the ginger. It's time for carrot soup.

Sometimes, the kitchen is a refuge.

Of course, the kitchen isn't automatically a trouble-free zone. Kitchen anxiety does exist, and all those knives and boiling pots mean it isn't always safe, either. But after spending a stressful day at work or at any time when life gets too complicated, I happily reach for my knife and lose myself in the simplicity of chopping carrots.

Carrots don't need feedback or negotiation, they don't break or require upgrading or get sick. They don't object to being peeled or want to weigh in on how finely they should be chopped. In short, carrots don't want anything from me. And like washing the dishes or putting away groceries, the straightforward ease of chopping vegetables is refreshing.

But the kitchen isn't always just refuge from something. It's also refuge in something. When I take refuge in the weight and warmth of sunlight as it brushes the kitchen windowsill, I'm somehow a little less burdened. Taking refuge in the food I'm working with, the color and texture and the sound of the knife hitting the chopping board, allows me to focus on something besides my worried preoccupations.

There's refuge, too, in the sensuous nature of cooking, the smells and sounds of a meal being made. The taste, of course, and the temperature and the bright orange color of a pile of freshly cut carrots.

Taking refuge is also the fact that I can spend time in this scrappy little kitchen, which I adore with its tiny stove and chipped linoleum floor. That the cupboards, for now, are full and I have the strength to stand on my own two feet at the chopping board. Taking refuge is an act of appreciation.

Is your kitchen ever a refuge? Do you turn to a particular recipe or task when you're distressed? Look up—what is there to appreciate right here, right now, right in front of your eyes?

Simple Carrot Soup for
Tumultuous Times

PEEL and chop one yellow onion. Sauté it in a pot with about a tablespoon of butter or olive oil over medium heat, stirring occasionally.

MEANWHILE, peel and chop enough carrots to equal roughly three times the amount of onion. When the onion is translucent, add the carrots and stir. Add a few pinches of salt.

FINELY chop a clove or two of garlic and set it aside. Finely chop a knob of ginger—thumb-size if this is a big pot of soup or if you really like ginger. Use half that amount for a smaller pot.

ADD the garlic and ginger to the pot and stir. After about a minute, add some water or stock (chicken or vegetable) to cover the vegetables by a good inch or so. Cover loosely and simmer gently until the carrots are very soft.

REMOVE the pot from the stove and let it cool for a few minutes.

IF you have a handheld blender, congratulations! You've made your life infinitely simpler. Use it now.

IF you don't have a handheld blender, no worries. Just use your food processor or blender to puree the soup. Be careful of the hot soup: You may have to do this in batches. When you're done, run out and buy yourself a handheld blender.

THIN the soup with more liquid, if needed, with more water or stock. You can use some milk, soy milk, or cream as well.

YOU can garnish the soup however you want, depending on what feels appropriate to your mood or pantry offerings: finely chopped herbs such as thyme or mint or rosemary; hot sauce, thinly sliced green onion, and a little toasted sesame oil; crème fraîche or sour cream and a sprinkle of lemon zest; toasted cumin seeds and a dash of smoked paprika; a drizzle of yogurt dusted with curry powder and a few sprigs of cilantro.

A Final Word on Meditation

MEDITATION is a tricky thing. We are often attracted to it mostly because of a mistaken notion that meditation will bring calmness and bliss to our hyperscheduled and confused lives. We believe that somehow we will shift from fifth gear into neutral just by folding our legs and counting our breath for 20 minutes. Somehow, our overworked and battered self will just melt into the warm embrace of repose and bliss.

This is a false promise, as anyone who has tried meditation knows. Sitting in stillness, with no social interaction, with none of the usual distractions to affirm our place in the universe, is often quite difficult. When the only thing we have to do is to focus on the rise and fall of our chest as we breathe, we are suddenly confronted with the unmediated, uncensored veracity of our thoughts. And even if we can get that under control, we may find that our bodies are achy and uncooperative to the point of great distraction. Or that we're antsy and restless.

Not that meditation can't be peaceful or even blissful at times. That certainly is possible and with time, perhaps even more so. Or maybe a better way to put it is that as we practice meditation, we develop a greater capacity for openness and resiliency. We can allow the world to come forth and express itself and be just what it is, and we can meet it in a way that doesn't diminish us or shut us down. Sometimes, this will feel peaceful and sometimes, this will feel rugged and impossible. And this will change from day to day, year to year, and even from moment to moment.

If meditation can promise anything, it is intimacy. Intimacy with the body and all the wisdom, secrets, pleasures, and pains it holds. Intimacy with the mind, with how it expresses the fundamental nature of who we are and how we function intellectually and emotionally. And, of course, intimacy with the physical world in which we dwell and, even more specifically, an intimacy with the sometimes simple, sometimes complex expression of the present moment.

The question then becomes, how intimate can we be? And further, what exactly is intimacy? What allows it to come forth and what holds it back? There are no set answers to these questions. We each need to explore and discover and ponder how we experience intimacy, what our relationship is to letting things in, to what we reject and what we call in closer. The simplicity of the form of meditation can allow us to experience this without the confusion and protectiveness of our usual thought processes.

What we find beneath the clutter of thoughts and ideas may or may not be peaceful. Maybe there will be a clutch of emotionality like grief or anger or even pleasure. Maybe there will be a well of creativity so deep and untapped that it will astonish. Or maybe it will be nothing special, just a random flutter of the mind at work, chugging away like a reliable old steam engine puffing along the tracks—a forgotten item on the grocery list, a memory of your grandmother, a solution to a thorny situation at work.

The secret to meditation (if there is indeed a secret!) is to do it as consistently as possible. Every day, in fact, or as close to every day as you can manage. This continuous coming back to your place, to what some describe as true home, builds a trust in the process that allows you to see deeper and deeper into your own inner workings. We begin to trust ourselves as well, and our capacity to hold and sort through the sometimes rough, sometimes glorious, often-changing truths of who we are.

The most important thing is to not do anything with or about these thoughts while in meditation. Maybe later you will act on them, and that's fine. But this time you have set aside for yourself is not about doing. Stay put. Stay in the stillness. Trust the stillness.

AFTERWORD

THE kitchen is often the last room in the house that I visit before bed. I like to wander about, checking the lock on the back door, filling the kettle, and setting out a mug for tomorrow's tea. There's always a few miscellaneous things to put away or a pile or two to straighten. Sometimes, I'm already thinking about tomorrow's meals and so I might pull something from the freezer, or make a note to pick up an ingredient.

I once went through a phase where I would start a small, fresh batch of yogurt nearly every night. In the evenings, just before bed, I would busy myself with gently heating the milk, pouring it into a bowl and stirring in the culture, covering it, and leaving it to sit overnight. The next morning, there it would be: the miracle of freshly made yogurt for breakfast. It was a nice ritual, and I remember appreciating those few quiet moments standing by the stove each evening, stirring the small pot of milk, and thinking about the day. (Note to self: Start making yogurt again.)

The kitchen is the most important place in my home.

My apartment is so small, the kitchen is nearly half of the square footage, so it naturally becomes the place where I spend most of my time. It is the anchor of my home; it is the anchor of my heart. I go to the kitchen when I want to feel the weight of this anchor, to have a visceral and very real sense of belonging and gratitude, of playfulness and appreciation. It is where I feed my friends and family, and it's where I am in turn fed in ways beyond the fuel for the belly. It is where I learn and reinforce the lessons of trust, gratitude, curiosity, and generosity. It is where I am most myself.

I hope this is true for you, too.

A Small Daily Bowl of Yogurt

2 cups whole milk

2 heaping tablespoons plain yogurt

IN a thick-bottomed pot over low heat, slowly warm the milk to about 190°F or so, stirring gently to prevent the milk from scorching. Remove it from the heat and pour into a medium bowl. This will help the mixture cool. Stir until the temperature comes down to 110° to 114°F. In the beginning, you may want to use a thermometer but, eventually, you will know when the temperature is right by touch alone.

PLACE the yogurt in a small bowl and whisk in some of the milk to thin it. Pour the yogurt mixture back into the remaining milk and stir to combine. Cover with a small plate that fits snugly over the top (or plastic wrap) and place the bowl in the oven with the heat turned off but the light turned on. Some people leave it on the counter, wrapped up in a thick towel and snuggled up with a hot-water bottle or on a heating pad turned on low. Much depends on how warm your house is or what season it is. The point here is to keep the yogurt as warm as possible, as yogurt needs to do its thing in the 110°F range.

COULD you make it easier on yourself and buy a yogurt maker? Yes. Could you make this more efficient and cook up several days' worth of yogurt in one batch? Yes. But the point here isn't to make things easier and quicker. Lord knows there's probably enough of that steely efficiency in your life already. The point is to find some quiet time, to enjoy the process, and to create a simple ritual that encourages presence and contemplation.

THE next day, remove the bowl from the oven and either enjoy the yogurt right away or put it in the refrigerator to chill.

WITH a deep bow of gratitude and respect to Nigel Slater for the inspiration.

ACKNOWLEDGMENTS

MY name is on this book but it truly (really truly) belongs to dozens of people.

First and foremost, to Jack and Lorrie Velden, my parents. My dad: the baker of cinnamon swirl bread, the pickler of cucumbers, the canner of homemade applesauce. It's been almost 15 years since I saw you last. I still miss you. My mum: an excellent home cook whose daily meals grew me up and who still inspires me with middle-of-the-week phone calls because there's a brilliant new soup recipe in the newspaper.

To my nieces, Sara and Jennie, who will carry on the legacy. I am grateful it is in good hands.

To Elissa Altman, who connected me to my agent, the amazing Sharon Bowers and to my wonderful editor at Rodale, Ursula Cary Ziemba. And by connected I mean she plugged me right in like a Christmas tree. Or should I say electric menorah?

To Ursula, my very first editor. You have been kind and gentle, patient and thorough. You have been perfect and I am very lucky. To Carol Angstadt and the rest of the team at Rodale for turning a bunch of messy pages into something beautiful, and to Sara Mulvanny for your lovely illustrations.

To Faith and Sara Kate of *The Kitchn* for seeing the diamond in me and finding a place for it to shine. And for Maxwell at *Apartment Therapy* for not making it hard to use my previously published work.

To Florence Caplow, my dearest friend and unfailing supporter. Twin lakes, deep and still: endless water stretching for miles, moonlight brilliant. Also, dharmista road trips, Umbrian lentils, and secret fund-raising campaigns.

To Scott and Ray who have been feeding me for years with grace and kinship. To Naomi Shihab Nye who, just once, encouraged me enough that I found a dot of confidence buried deep inside me. That's all it took: the tiny dot and the finding of it. To Deborah Madison for so much: your writing, your food, your friendship, and for making it possible for me to spend some time beneath the vast blue skies of New Mexico.

To Katharine Shields for your guidance on how to live in the dark and in the light. You always inspire, even when you think you don't. To Renshin Bunce who helped me to find poetry at the farmers' market and comfort and joy at the bra shop. To Siobhan for the plum pud and lasting friendship. To John Gruenwald for what once was and for the friendship it has become.

To Karissa Sellman for the camera that opened up my world and to Dana Elliot who did likewise by making it possible for me to buy a decent computer. To Anne Louise Hoffman for stealth Good Eggs deliveries and brilliant ideas, and to David Woolman for sustaining me with rides to the grocery store, good friendship, and endless bowls of ramen. To my friends and sangha at the San Francisco Zen Center and to the many Zen cooks who have taught me there. To Paul Haller, for being my teacher, even when you're not.

To my fellow dwellers in Avontopia: Aya and Coreay and baby Miya; Adriana and the boys; Clark and Eve; Ben and Robin and Zeus the Wonder Dog; and especially to Alice who has made it possible for me to live in paradise. (And for those occasional deliveries of tortillas wrapped in brown paper from El Molino Central.)

To the Richmond sitting group whose dana (teacher donation) literally put food on my table some of the months spent writing this and whose questions and observations on their practice always deepens my own. To the workers at Pizzaiolo's morning program whose coffee and yogurt and granola (and doughnuts!) fueled many chapters of this book. To the cooks and food community of Oakland, California: may our vision of making good food available to everyone continue to flourish and may justice and sovereignty prevail.

And finally, to all the friends and angels who gave freely of their support, advice, guidance, encouragement, enthusiasm: Dianne Jacob, Rachel Cole, Carrie Sullivan, Mimi Saunders, Lee Lipp, Susan O'Connell, Anna Thorn, Daigan Gaither, Connie Stoops, Julia Allenby, Judith Randall, Jennie Schact, Kathy Keller, Kathryn Gilmore, Mary Muszynski, Ray Arata, Sherri Nordwall, Marie Martin, Samin Nosrat, Erin Scott, Tara Austin Weaver. I know I am forgetting many. Please forgive me.

INDEX

Cooking (cont.)
posture during, 76–78
practice and, 101, 169–70
presence and, 57–59
proficiency in, 133–34
repetitiveness of, 19–20,
131–32
seasons and, 38
senses and, 85–87
as solace during difficult
times, 196–98
techniques (See Techniques)
tools (See Equipment)
unambitiousness in,
222–23
well-functioning kitchen
and, 60–61
Cooks, two kinds of, 235–36
Cosmopolitan magazine, 139
Counting of precious moments
and things, 233–34

D

Dairy Hollow House Cookbook, The
(book), 150
Difficult times, kitchen as
solace during, 196–98
Dinner, suggestions for simple,
182–83
Dishes, washing, 97–98
Dissatisfaction, indicators of,
84
Distressing situations
in the kitchen, 103–4
kitchen as solace during,
196–98
Dragonwagon, Crescent
(author), 150
Drudgery, 97–98, 130–32
Duty, 130–32

E

Ego, in the kitchen, 222
Energy
anger and, 160–61
increasing in the kitchen,
143
redirecting restless, 196
Enlightenment, intimacy and,
115

Entertaining
being prepared for, 193–95
as a gift, 202
hospitality and, 188–90
Equilibrioception, 85
Equipment
appliances, 68–69
cutting boards, 36
kitchen happiness and,
34–35
knives, 36
pots and pans, 74–75
rule for acquiring, 73
timers, 88–90
Experience, value of in cooking,
86–87, 100–102
Experiences
being available to, 57–59
grounding activities, 24
integrating
soji and, 65
while resting, 80–81
openness to, 114–16

F

Fear
of failure, 144–49
of impermanence, 62
of mortality, 103–4
Fearlessness, 144–45
Feet, cooking and, 77–78
Fierceness, kitchens as places
of, 96
Freedom, 36, 146
Friendliness, hospitality and,
189
Frustration
guilt and, 172
as indicator of dissatisfaction,
84
with other people, 245
releasing in the kitchen,
179–81

G

Generosity
as basic stance of hospitality,
189
gift giving and, 205
inner agility and, 168